THE SOUL *of an* ORGANIZATION

UNDERSTANDING THE VALUES THAT DRIVE SUCCESSFUL CORPORATE CULTURES

RICHARD S. GALLAGHER

Dearborn™
Trade Publishing
A **Kaplan Professional** Company

TO COLLEEN, the light of my life—and to the spirit of the ideal corporate culture, in Psalms 15:2.

Vice President and Publisher: Cynthia A. Zigmund
Editorial Director: Donald J. Hull
Senior Acquisitions Editor: Jean Iversen
Senior Managing Editor: Jack Kiburz
Interior Design: Lucy Jenkins
Cover Design: Design Solutions
Typesetting: the dotted i

Published by Dearborn Trade Publishing
A Kaplan Professional Company

Library of Congress Cataloging-in-Publication Data

Gallagher, Richard S.
  The soul of an organization : understanding the values that drive successful corporate cultures / Richard S. Gallagher.
    p.   cm.
  Includes bibliographical references and index.
  ISBN 0-7931-5780-3 (pbk.)
  1. Corporate culture.   2. Organizational effectiveness.   3. Corporate culture—Case studies.   I. Title.
  HD58.7 .G345 2003
  658—dc21

                                                                    2002009282

"In *The Soul of an Organization,* Rich Gallagher presents the essential role corporate culture plays in the success of any business. The concept is made clear through real-life examples from thriving companies, including many we all know and recognize. *The Soul of an Organization* is a must-read for any executive looking to evolve their organization's culture into a strategic advantage."

Carolyn Healey, Founder and Publisher, supportindustry.com, crmindustry.com, and RecognizeServiceExcellence.com

"Many studies have shown that high customer satisfaction helps drive revenue and shareholder value. This book shows readers how to create a culture where every employee feels he or she can positively impact customer satisfaction and loyalty. Great reading!"

Scott Bajtos, Group Vice President, Customer Advocacy, Business Objects

"I read everything that Rich Gallagher writes, but *The Soul of an Organization* really caught my attention. Rich has unraveled the mysteries of corporate culture that so few of us really understand. I found myself saying 'Gee, I never thought about that' over and over again as I learned more about this critical success factor to any organization. This book has got to be on every working manager's bookshelf."

Bill Rose, Founder and CEO, Service and Support Professionals Association (SSPA)

Contents

Introduction

This book has one purpose—to show how your values, and not your business practices, are what drive your success. In a world where 98 percent of organizations are fixated on the mechanics of their businesses, knowing this secret is perhaps the most strategic competitive factor in today's marketplace. These values, which nowadays we often refer to by the moniker "corporate culture," are not just sterile, 20,000-foot-high concepts for upper management; they are the keys to empower workplaces of any size to succeed at a level far beyond what most people imagine.

WHO THIS BOOK IS FOR

In *The Soul of an Organization,* we bring home the concepts of understanding and managing these values to people who lead work groups of any size, including:

- Frontline and operations managers who want to make substantial improvements in productivity, morale, costs, and turnover

- Leaders of customer contact organizations who want to create a quantum increase in their service quality
- Human resources and corporate training professionals who want to move from simple employee development to transforming their cultures
- Senior management who want to dramatically change their organization's bottom line by rallying their people around a clear sense of purpose

Having the "right" values sounds like the most natural thing in the world, but in reality, managing around values rather than business processes succeeds precisely because it runs counter to what most of us call human nature. For example, let's compare some common misconceptions about daily business life with the best practices of strong corporate cultures:

- You can't create great service simply by exhorting people to be nice, but when you design systems around responding directly to customers, like Dell Computer does, you create industry-leading customer satisfaction levels.
- You can't create productivity by constantly holding a stopwatch to people, which in fact breeds little more than sullen compliance. But when a company like Southwest Airlines instills a near fanatical devotion to teamwork in everything it does, it breeds a level of productivity that is nearly double that of its competitors.
- You don't demonstrate leadership just by telling people what to do. But when you invest in training at a level far above that of your competitors, like insurance giant USAA does, you produce a workforce where 40 percent of your people get promoted every year and barely 5 percent leave—in an industry where these numbers are often reversed.

In cases such as these and others, your culture is ultimately determined by how you respond to each of the hundreds of business decisions you make every day. *And each of these decisions is governed either by human nature or by core values that transcend human nature.*

WHAT YOU WILL FIND IN THIS BOOK

In the chapters that follow, you will learn how this conscious decision to transcend human nature is often the single common thread running between firms who dominate their markets and workplaces that stand out within their organizations. In the process, you will see things such as leadership, motivation, customer service, quality, and success in a light you have never seen them in before.

Chapter 1 starts with a look at what business culture is—and more important, what it is not—and why it has such a strong influence on your success. It examines some real-life examples of how values drive successful businesses, explores common myths about values and corporate culture, and provides a self-test that allows you to assess your own workplace practices against current best practices. This test forms the cornerstone of the material that follows and will help you focus on how best to understand and strengthen your own culture.

Chapters 2 through 8 delve further into these best practices, as seen through the eyes of seven core traits that drive modern business culture. Each of these chapters presents profiles of specific organizations that practice these core traits, including Vanguard, Dell Computer, Wendy's, and Cirque du Soleil:

1. *The Strategists,* who create systems that drive operational excellence
2. *The Motivators,* who succeed by creating a positive working environment that promotes respect, autonomy, and personal growth
3. *The Team Builders,* who are devoted to creating a strong team environment, starting from recruiting all the way through building strong internal relationships in the workplace
4. *The Nimble,* who embrace change as an opportunity and can adapt their cultures to shifts in markets, technology, demographics, and other factors
5. *The Customer Champions,* who focus on putting the customer at the front of every business decision they make
6. *The Passionates,* who see their work as a mission and a way of life and infect everyone around them with this sense of mission

7. *The Visionaries,* who lead by setting goals that make everyone on their team part of something greater than themselves

Many of these values seem self-evident in theory, but as this book explores how real businesses succeed or fail at putting them into practice, you will understand that a predictable split exists between human nature and reaching for higher goals. No one wakes up every morning planning to run a "bad" workplace, but when human nature wins out, that is often exactly what they get. Once you understand the mechanics of this, you can chart your own personal track that leads you over and above your competition.

Chapter 9 looks at the dynamics of how business cultures evolve over time, and why they succeed and fail. Chapter 10 takes this a step further and explores how your cultural values can be the most important factor in the success or failure of mergers, acquisitions, and other forms of business expansion. In Chapter 11, we close with perhaps the most important point of all—how existing business cultures, including your own culture, can grow and change for the better.

For me personally, the journey leading to this book began back in the 1980s, as part of a five-person start-up company that set out to create a total service culture as well as a great software product. We grew to become a major firm that went public on the Nasdaq stock market. More important, we created a strong workplace where people bought in to what we were doing and looked forward to coming to work in the morning.

In later years, as a consultant and in management, I've seen the same process work over and over: core values, combined with a genuine respect for people, taking businesses to heights they never dreamed of. These firms see both themselves and their customers with a clarity afforded to few others, and they exploit this clarity as a dominant advantage in the marketplace. It is a magical experience shared by only a few people in today's business world, and you are about to join the club. Enjoy!

RICHARD S. GALLAGHER

Acknowledgments

I'd like to thank the following people who provided reviews, background information, interviews, or other assistance: Molly Faust of American Express; Mark Campagnolo of The Boatyard Grill; Jeffrey Burness, Kate Lunde, Roger Morehouse, and Lisa Patz of The CBORD Group; Nedjma Belbahri of Cirque du Soleil; Pam Selker Rak of Communitech; Marianne Loewe and Dennis Garvey of Concern America; Dave Messing of Continental Airlines; Jeff Hanavan of Cornell University; Dell Corporate Public Relations; John Walker of <www.fourmilab.ch>; John Moody and Madeline Klosterman of Fox News Channel; Mark Monseau and Gerri Battista of Johnson & Johnson; Peggy Rivers of the New York State Department of Education; Douglas Daly of Outback Steakhouse; Melanie Jones of Southwest Airlines; Carolyn Healey of Supportindustry.com; Jo Natale of Wegmans; and Jeff Coghlan, Joan Comerford, and Tricia Morehouse of Wendcentral.

My lifelong interest in workplace culture was first sparked many years ago by the incredible experiences I had with growth technology organizations. I am particularly indebted to three people who not only mentored me but seemingly created hundreds of jobs and millions of dollars out of thin air by fostering a sense of excellence—Lou Crain, John Swanson, and my own father, the late Dr. Richard H. Gallagher.

I feel that Jean Iversen, my editor at Dearborn Trade Publishing, has helped Dearborn become one of the industry's most respected business trade publishers while keeping true to a vision of improving life in the workplace. It has been an honor and a pleasure to work with Jean, senior editorial assistant Sandy Thomas, senior managing editor Jack Kiburz, and everyone else on Dearborn's editorial and production team.

I would also like to acknowledge the love and support of my family and friends, and especially thank my wife, Colleen, for her role in this project. Aside from our still being madly in love with each other after nearly 30 years together, she is the best editorial assistant and sounding board one could possibly have. Thank you for cheering on one of my greatest pleasures one more time.

1

Understanding Your Business Culture

In May of 1979, at the start of a busy Memorial Day weekend, an air tragedy riveted the world's attention. An American Airlines DC-10 lost its right-wing engine on takeoff from Chicago's O'Hare Airport and crashed seconds later in a fireball, killing all 271 people aboard. This accident, which eventually led to grounding all DC-10 aircraft for more than a month, was later traced to problems with an engine maintenance procedure developed by American's own mechanics.

Nearly a generation later, on May 11, 1996, another air tragedy dominated the media. ValuJet flight 592, a jetliner carrying 110 people, plunged nose first into the Florida Everglades after a fire broke out in its cargo hold, killing all aboard. This time, an investigation discovered that mislabeled oxygen canisters loaded by a third-party maintenance contractor had ignited, causing the crash.

The aftermath of these two incidents could not have been more different for the business fortunes of these carriers. American, rated at the time as the number one airline for customer satisfaction, did not experience any long-term drop in revenue after its accident. On the other hand, ValuJet, a start-up low-fare carrier long under fire for its labor practices and maintenance procedures, found itself grounded—and shortly afterwards changed its name by acquiring low-fare rival AirTran Airways. The telling lesson here is that one carrier with a strong service culture survived a tragedy that *was* its fault, while another carrier that lacked one was quickly forced out of the skies following an accident that *was not* its fault.

So what does the fate of two major airlines have to do with your own business, workplace, or other organization? Plenty. For them, success or failure hinged on underlying core values, which, in turn, drove their daily business decisions. The same is true for you and your business, and many people in business today never realize what a dramatic impact these values can have on their own success in the marketplace. Let's look at one example that shows how even the smallest businesses need the right values to survive and flourish.

A TALE OF TWO FARMERS MARKETS

Years ago, I once stopped at a large farmers market on the outskirts of a town in Pennsylvania. Nobody said hello, and most of the help just sat there and stared as I walked in. Trying to find some tomatoes ripe enough to use for dinner that night, I picked through about a dozen before a surly farmer strolled over and drawled, "Boy, you gonna eat those tomatoes or frame 'em?" More recently, I came back to town and found this market now boarded up and out of business.

This market was part of a farm that had existed since the 1700s, and if you were to ask the farmers why the market went under, they would probably talk angrily about how they could no longer compete in a world of 24-hour supermarkets and tight profit margins. But if they were to get into their cars and drive a few hours north to another farmers market in a small central New York town, they would find hundreds of people crowding to get in every week. This farmers market offers lots of fresh produce, along with the sounds of strolling musicians, the smell of fresh-baked pastries and ethnic foods, local arts and crafts, friendly people, and the feel of a community gathering place. And despite gleaming new chain food stores down the road, business is booming at this farmers market, with no signs of slowing down.

Situations like these underscore that in business, as with life itself, the deeper values of *who you are* become vastly more important than *what happens to you.* But in daily work life, most businesses focus on the latter and pay scant attention to the former. They worry about their production schedules, their deadlines, their competition, and their financing, but they rarely look inward at themselves. That's why, when you ask most people what their workplace culture is like, they look at you quizzically and say, "Well, we're here to work, aren't we?" But this intangible thing that most people never talk about, this gestalt that we call "business culture," may perhaps be the most important factor in the growth and survival of any business. Understand this fact, and you can reach levels of success that are unimaginable for most people.

DEFINING BUSINESS CULTURE

The dictionary defines culture as "the customary beliefs, social forms, and material traits of a racial, religious, or social group." It is derived from the same linguistic roots as the word *cult,* itself taken from the Latin term *to adore.* In an organizational setting, the meaning of culture extends to the core beliefs, behaviors, and actions behind its daily business life.

Every workplace has a culture all its own, one that may be good, bad, or indifferent. As often as not, its values are unspoken, but they exert a powerful influence on the behavior of those who choose to be part of that organization. Their tenets help people self-select the groups they want to be associated with—the hipsters who start a media firm, the suit-clad accountant who goes to Wall Street, and the deeply spiritual person who joins a nonprofit social agency are all influenced by this tacit sense of culture. And while rarely discussed openly, it is nonetheless extraordinarily powerful. Its core values are a conforming influence that change only with great effort and consensus, and self-perpetuate themselves even as companies grow to include thousands of people spread across the globe. It is nothing less than the soul of an organization.

So, what exactly is a business culture? Let's take a look at some of the things that it is and, more important, is not:

A business culture is . . .	A business culture is not . . .
Your values and beliefs	Your products and services
Generally unspoken	Promoted externally
Your style	Your policies and procedures
The types of people you hire	Your recruiting process
What behaviors you reward	What behaviors you say you want

Much of what forms your business culture is neither good nor bad. It simply defines the context of who you are, and that context then drives your day-to-day actions in the marketplace. One company may be casual with loud rock music blaring, and another may be buttoned-down and professional—and both may be successful companies. One may have a generous refund policy, another may pinch every penny—and again, both may be successful within their own niches. It is when the values of a business culture conflict with larger values in life, such as respect for employees, fair treatment of customers, or business ethics, that problems can arise. Conversely, the development of strong business culture values can often lead people to transcend both their competition and their marketplace. For example, one restaurateur in a small upstate New York town has proved repeatedly that when you create the right system of values, crowds naturally follow you.

THE SYSTEM BEHIND A WORLD-CLASS RESTAURANT

Ithaca, New York, is a college town of less than 100,000 people—a place where you would not normally invest $2 million to build a spectacular 200-seat waterfront restaurant with more than 100 employees. But to local restaurateur Mark Campagnolo and his partners, this unprecedented gamble was no gamble at all. Even though the restaurant does almost no advertising other than word of mouth, lines of customers stream out the door of **The Boatyard Grill** every weekend, and sometimes a three-hour wait for tables is not unheard of.

As a former chain restaurant executive, Mark got to see firsthand what worked well in successful restaurants. In the late 1980s, he used this experience to transform a sleepy, long-closed family Italian restaurant in Ithaca into one of the top 300 private restaurants in America. He saw where breaking the mold of most large multiunit operations represented an opportunity to succeed on a grander scale, and The Boatyard Grill represented an opportunity to put these ideas into practice from scratch.

First and foremost, Mark runs a tight ship. Members of his waitstaff spend more than a week in training classes, complete with lectures, videos, tests, and practice sessions, before they ever get near an actual diner. Strong operating procedures are in place for everything, from how soon a customer is greeted to when a customer receives the check and change, and managers are on the floor at all times. More important is Mark's philosophy, where employee and guest relationships govern over the usual "numbers" that drive most food-service operations. "We're based on certain values, and our principal one is to build guest loyalty rather than maximize the average check. A lot of things that make us who we are aren't in a policy manual. Waitstaff check on each other's tables. People will walk customers to their cars with umbrellas when it's raining. We even stock little flashlights and inexpensive reading glasses up front for elderly people who may have trouble reading the menu in our soft lighting."

Above all, Mark looks out for his employees. Many people on Mark's team have worked with him for years, while others have left with hefty pensions. Today, there is even more of a focus on career paths at the new Boatyard facility, where promising employees have the opportunity to become shift leaders, trainers, or managers. And it's not unusual to find the whole team going to Buffalo together for an NFL football game, or groups of employees hanging out at the restaurant off-hours as paying customers themselves.

The end result is a restaurant where people genuinely enjoy taking good care of their customers, from big things like special occasions to little ones like remembering what a customer ordered last time. According to Mark, "Above all, we try to get everyone past the idea that a customer is a transaction. When you feel that way, it shows in everything else you do."

Understanding your core values, and putting them into practice, truly produces a hidden profit margin. The Boatyard Grill doesn't just do a little better than other restaurants in the area, it completely blows them away. Is it because of its food? Mark Campagnolo is the first to admit that the Boatyard isn't what you would call a fine-dining establishment. "We even have kids' meals and fishermen's platters on our menu, not exactly what you'd find with haute cuisine." How about a brand-new facility? Mark previously transformed an old, brick family restaurant built in 1932 to one of the top restaurants in the country. Most diners at The Boatyard Grill will tell you that it simply feels different at his restaurant. They feel special there, people take good care of them, and they have a great time—and they return over and over. It is a formula based on best practices that you'll never see on their menu.

Very few firms have a business culture department. For all its importance to your business, you can't simply look in a specific place and find it. Look critically at each of the workplaces you have been involved with in your own career. It is likely that they all had deep, ingrained values that governed their way of doing business. These might have been good values such as diversity, respect, hard work, and frontline authority, to name a few. They also might have been counterproductive values such as parochialism, mistrust of employees, and command-and-control decision making. Either way, these firms undoubtedly had strong values—and in all likelihood, these values were not only unwritten, but unspoken as well. In most workplaces, you rarely hear these values discussed openly. People simply demonstrate them in the way they do their jobs every day.

While the values behind a business culture may not be well documented, they are certainly well understood. It is a tradition that is maintained by example in most cases. These values are passed along with unmistakable certainty from coworker to coworker, and manager to employee, in the form of each of the many daily work-life decisions that form our jobs. At a more global level, these values are transmitted by the decisions made at the top of an organization. And compared with formal pronouncements such as mission or vision statements, it is within these exchanges that the *real* culture is passed along.

The simple fact is that you already have a business culture, even if you are a small family business, and this culture may be much more important to your success than the factors you normally think about. Businesses with poor cultures have failed despite offering great products and balance sheets, and ones with great cultures have prevailed under much more difficult circumstances. By understanding and managing your own culture, you have a better chance to play to your strengths—or change your weaknesses.

So, in a world where there are few "business culture departments," how do you get your arms around the concept of this culture? And how do you put it to work to improve the success and morale of your own workplace? Perhaps the best place to start lies in examining how much organizational behavior has in common with human behavior in general. In many ways, business culture parallels human culture:

- It is a badge of identity for the members of a group.
- It serves a greater good.
- It supports long-term goals.
- It can change as a result of major life events.
- It transcends the individual.

Above all, both business and human cultures are part of humanity's lifelong efforts to create systems that predictably influence human behavior. If you look critically at firms that enjoy lasting success in the marketplace, you will often find core values that, in turn, drive their day-to-day operations. They may be intangible, but you can practically sense them as you walk around the workplaces of these firms. *And when you consciously understand and manage the core values of your own workplace, you gain the ability to succeed at a level far beyond the majority of organizations that do not.*

STRONG VALUES TURN EVEN SMALL BUSINESSES INTO GREAT BUSINESSES

One afternoon, more than two decades ago, my wife and I went apartment hunting in suburban Seattle. We happened to tour one complex along with a polite young man who had just moved to the area, and we asked him what he did for a living. He smiled and said sheepishly, "I work for a start-up company that you've probably never heard of. It's called Microsoft. We have a handful of employees nowadays, and I helped write a product of theirs called Microsoft Basic." A generation later, Microsoft—which had its roots as a small company known as Traf-o-Data, writing software to control traffic signals—has now become one of the world's largest corporations. And our friend probably no longer lives in a $400-per-month apartment in Bellevue, Washington.

The majority of today's large businesses were once small businesses, but ones with very clear visions of who they were and where they were headed. While not every small business grows as big as Microsoft, and many would not want to, this common denominator appears in nearly every successful firm that started small. Their values as small businesses had a major influence on whether they had the opportunity to become larger. Now, let's turn the situation around and look at the attitudes behind a computer firm that failed despite the hottest personal computer market in history and the backing of a large multinational corporation. A chance encounter a few years ago gave me a rare chance to see the impact of this organization's corporate culture for myself.

THE ZOMBIES NEXT DOOR

I had purchased a laptop computer made by a firm whose view of service was consistently shoddy at best. It advertised a 24-hour overnight replacement policy, but when my CD-ROM drive broke, I was told, "Sorry, we're all out of replacements. You'll have to wait three weeks." When I had complex technical problems (I am a very savvy computer user), indifferent support representatives would tell me in a monotone to reload Windows and hang up. Even their supervisors were like zombies. It always seemed like people never gave so much as a moment of thought to my problems before pushing me off the phone with a bad answer.

So one night, I was looking at the manual for this product—by now, the only real resource that I had to turn to—and happened to notice this company's address. It was strangely familiar. In fact, it was on the same street as a software firm that happened to be one of my major consulting clients. On my next trip to visit them on the West Coast, I came in to work and saw that the two firms actually shared a common parking lot!

The next morning, I made it a point to come in bright and early, staked out a window, and just sat there and watched as employees from the two companies came in to work for the day. People from my client's firm walked tall, waved hello to people in the parking lot, and smiled and joked with each other as they walked in to work. Meanwhile, the other firm's employees trudged in silently, many with their eyes focused on the ground and their shoulders hunched. They looked like convicts marching off to jail.

I have no idea what things were like inside the walls of that company. But taking a look at my own service experiences, and then holding them up against the looks on the employees' faces, my perception was that both employees and service were unwanted costs, to be reduced wherever possible. And indeed, this company succeeded in reducing these costs to zero, because it exited the computer business shortly afterwards.

If there is one common denominator in both of these stories, it is that business practices matter, but business culture matters even more. The computer firm that failed had a reasonably good product, a state-of-the-art call center, and the backing of one of the world's largest companies. But it went down in flames because it couldn't engage the hearts and minds of the people who worked there—and customers noticed. I personally will never again buy *any* product made by this corporation, because its computer division consistently violated my trust. Conversely, Microsoft has long been recognized as a strong investor in customer-service infrastructure, from online knowledge bases to state-of-the-art ergonomics in its workplaces. Values like these are part of the real secret behind how a small group of people created a multibillion-dollar empire from scratch.

FIVE MYTHS ABOUT BUSINESS CULTURE

As important as your culture is, it remains one of the most misunderstood concepts in business today. People often confuse it with more specific things, such as internal policies and procedures, or dismiss it altogether as a "soft science." For this reason, strong cultures may be common among leading firms, but they remain rare among businesses as a whole. Let's take a look at some of the most frequent misperceptions that surround the subject of your business culture.

Myth #1: Culture Means Putting Your Values in a Mission Statement

Try an experiment some time. Make a list of the companies that have given you terrible customer service over the past year, and then look up their mission statements. In all likelihood, most of them will express values that are directly in conflict with the experience you received from these firms. In fact, you may have a similar experience to what one university president experienced several years ago, when his board of trustees asked him to develop a mission statement for his school. He surveyed the mission statements of dozens of other universities and made an amazing discovery—they were almost all exactly the same. But the schools behind them certainly were not! Very often, judging the culture of an organization from its mission statement is similar to judging a product's quality by its advertising slogans.

When author Stephen Covey proposed the concept of a mission statement in his groundbreaking book *Seven Habits of Highly Effective People,* it was intended to help organizations develop a purpose and scope for their daily actions. For some organizations that sincerely practiced what he preached, the development of a mission statement accomplished its goals. But as the concept became elevated to rock-star status during the 1990s, every business soon had to have a mission statement. And if you compare many of these mission statements to actual behavior, it often became an egregious case of management-by-slogan that had little or no effect on business reality in the trenches.

Strong cultures don't necessarily need a mission statement, but they need a *mission,* an idea that inspires people to be part of something greater than themselves. For example, when man first started to explore space, this captivated the public—and motivated thousands of scientists and engineers to join workplaces that accomplished what had never been done before. Or, on a smaller scale, imagine a well-liked and trusted local dentist who has been in practice for 25 years. He has no mission statement, and in a sense, no need of one. His core values involve being honest and straightforward and not practicing "sales dentistry." Putting these values into a public statement would probably sound hollow and self-serving, like saying, "I don't beat my wife." But he has no misconceptions about what these values are, and lives them in his daily work. As a result, he has a thriving practice built on word-of-mouth clients. Both these scientists, and this dentist, have missions.

Do you and your employees need to understand the core values behind your culture? Absolutely. Is it a good idea to write them down? Sure, if that helps everyone understand these values. But don't confuse this very important need with crafting a mission statement, which is a public statement that defines your business purpose. And don't ever make the mistake of thinking that a mission statement alone will define or change your culture.

Myth #2: Culture Is Mainly an Issue for Larger Businesses

By virtue of its very name, the term *business culture* often implies the environment of a large corporation. Perhaps as a result of this, many small businesses often don't stop to realize that they have a business culture, and the effect that this culture has on their bottom line. Let's take a look at one successful marketing agency and how its values of being technically savvy and responsive defined its success in the marketplace.

FROM THE BASEMENT TO THE BIG TIME

Few businesses started smaller than Pittsburgh's **Communitech.** For Pam Selker Rak, her dream of a high-tech public relations firm started in the basement of her house, shortly after breaking away from the latest in a series of corporate marketing jobs. But there were core traits that set her apart from the average marketing writer. For one thing, she produced quickly—it wasn't unusual for her to complete a project or place an article almost as soon as it was assigned. Moreover, she made it a point to speak her clients' language, which in her case meant going from a journalism background to understanding hardcore computer networking and software applications. She even hired a professional cartoonist to help position her business in the marketplace, inventing a "virtual employee" by the name of Marc Com (after a common industry shorthand for "marketing communications").

Today, Rak's firm has grown to become a major regional agency. Communitech was recently voted Business of the Week as one of the area's up-and-coming firms, Rak herself was recently honored as one of the top 50 businesswomen in Pennsylvania, and her firm now counts giants such as IBM, Bayer, and Cornell University among its clients. And the company still knows what TCP/IP means.

Rak and her company work in an environment that is dominated by large ad agencies and public relations firms. She manages to use this to her advantage, however, by being responsive and tapping a niche market where clients need her expertise in thinking like them. Instead of trying unsuccessfully to be another national ad agency, she succeeds by knowing clearly who she is—a strong marketing partner for the technology community—and doing it better than anyone else.

Sadly, culture works against small businesses more often than it works for them. Large corporations, particularly in service businesses such as retail and food service, often invest in training people to reinforce a common sense of who they are. So, for example, while the proprietor of a small business may hesitate to give a customer a refund when there is a problem, an entry-level person at McDonald's or Best Buy would probably take care of the same problem without a moment's hesitation. Small businesses must often understand that the humblest frontline employees of many national chains know more, and often a lot more, about service than they do.

The same is true of the working environment of smaller organizations. For instance, a young relative of mine recently took a job at the dining hall of a small private college and left after less than one week. During that week, she saw cooks constantly yelling at everyone, people refusing to help each other, and even a mass walkout by the dishwashers after one of them was spit on by a student and managers did nothing about it. Of three new employees hired that week, only one was still there by the end of the week. I later asked a colleague in the food-service business how things could get this bad and expected to hear about issues such as lack of management training, limited career options, or low pay. Instead, he said simply, "We have a system behind what we do. Our system would never allow things like this to happen. They don't have a system." More accurately, they don't have a sense of what is wrong with their own culture.

Myth #3: Business Culture Is Relatively Static

We tend to think of most businesses as monolithic entities. In reality, they often involve groups of individual cultures and subcultures, which may or may not behave according to larger principles. On a day-to-day basis, what people perceive about your business can vary from person to person, from work group to work group, or, as in the case that follows, from location to location.

CHAINS DON'T ALWAYS EQUAL CONSISTENCY

There is a chain restaurant with several locations in the area where I live. Visiting one of its restaurants one day, my wife and I stood waiting for what seemed like an eternity for one of the many employees flitting by to make even eye contact with us. Once we were finally seated, a waitress stopped by ten minutes later, acting like she wanted to be a million miles away. We placed our orders, and after another long wait, a couple of burnt sandwiches were dropped off without a word.

The same week, we went to another branch of the same restaurant, 20 miles away. Here, we were greeted immediately, a friendly waitress took our order at once, and we were served food cooked to perfection. While we were eating, I couldn't help but notice that the manager was quite visible on the floor, making small talk, pitching in, and encouraging everyone on the team.

Does this chain have a culture? I don't know. It has a menu. But each of these individual restaurants certainly has its own culture. And if you ask practically anyone I know, they will tell you that they generally avoid the first restaurant and like the second one—and, in general, there is an amazingly consistent "group think" that develops from individual experiences. As a result, consistent success often depends on how well you can maintain consistent values in every corner of your organization.

Myth #4: Good Cultures Are Invariably Successful

You can make a good case that a strong business culture is one of the most important factors in your success. At the same time, it is one of many other factors that drive your business. If you decide to open a restaurant that specializes in serving fried possum, no amount of business culture may guarantee your success. Conversely, if you offer a product or service that sets the market on fire, you may succeed even without the best values in the world—at least in the short term. Here are some of the factors that mitigate the impact of your business culture:

Sometimes the bad guys win. While many, if not most, market leaders have strong cultures, there are also firms that succeed despite poor service or labor problems. When it seems like some companies flourish despite the feelings of their customers and their employees, other factors often are at work. These may include better products, better services, a more competitive price point, or market leadership in a new technology area.

Perhaps most telling is that as companies like these succeed in the marketplace, their cultures often improve with the growth of the company. In perhaps the same way that some political insurgents become statesmen as their causes prevail, some firms do whatever it takes to succeed at first and then build on their successes by developing a more sustainable, lasting culture.

Being a good guy isn't enough. The landmark 1980s book *In Search of Excellence* profiled numerous firms that succeeded in the marketplace by getting close to their customers, and their employees. A decade later, a significant number of these firms faced financial troubles as competition or changing market conditions disrupted their business models. In a similar vein, several companies that have won the Malcolm Baldridge Award, America's highest honor for providing quality, have found that the award was no guarantee of market success in future years. And, unfortunately, the same is true for some firms that were once lauded for their business cultures.

Firms with great cultures and poor products, or weak marketing, or insufficient capital, can still fail in the harsh glare of the marketplace. What is telling, however, is how much more latitude organizations have when they have good cultures. Studies show that they retain customers and employees longer, spend less on marketing, and even have higher market values compared with similar firms. To succeed in the long term, these advantages must be paired with the right products, services, and business models. No business can ultimately defy the laws of supply and demand.

Cultures can change. Life is change, and these changes frequently affect the culture of an organization. Trends in society evolve, markets shift, and key people come and go. Moreover, what worked for a company in the past may no longer fit the present reality.

Organizations make choices every day that affect their culture, and these changes knowingly or unknowingly guide their business fortunes in the future. For example, a small local vegetarian restaurant in upstate New York decided early on to seek a national soapbox for its recipes and workplace philosophy, and eventually the Moosewood Collective became one of the world's most recognized names in vegetarian cookbooks. Conversely, another local restaurant with dreams of expansion let its food and service quality slip as it grew, and went quickly from having lines out the door to closing for good. In both cases, these businesses started with a specific culture at a particular point in time and moved on as circumstances changed.

Each of these issues underscores the fact that businesses are not driven by their culture alone. Success in today's marketplace is, and always has been, driven by a complex web of competitive factors. To prevail in the long term, an organization needs to keep on top of its overall business environment, and must be flexible enough to react to changes in the market. At the same time, your culture combines with the other success factors that drive your business—and in many cases, ultimately transcends them.

Myth #5: Business Culture Is a "Soft Skill"

There are still leaders today who believe that corporate culture is one of those "soft" concepts that has little bearing on their bottom line. Some of these businesses would sooner send their employees on a spiritual enlightenment retreat than look critically at their corporate culture. As a result, they give scant attention to what is often one of the most powerful forces shaping their business destiny. Conversely, for many leading organizations, culture is the place where they start—including one of the world's elite military units.

THE U.S. MARINES: The Culture Behind "the Few and the Proud"

Few organizations are less touchy-feely than the **United States Marine Corps.** But according to a study led by McKinsey consultant Jason Santamaria, the Corps serves as a model for developing a culture that inspires and motivates its frontline employees. Some of its practices that translate to the business world include:

- *Developing core values:* Marine training is 12 weeks long and isn't aimed at developing job skills. It focuses almost exclusively on instilling its core tenets of honor, courage, and commitment. Similarly, the Marines' Officer Candidates School in Quantico, Virginia, spends ten weeks teaching future platoon leaders the logistics and management theories behind leading a military team.

- *Preparing every person to lead:* In battle situations, every person must be prepared to take a leadership role. For example, the Marines extensively cross-train people to be able to perform any function within a four-person fire group during its infantry training, and rotate a team's duties among people to create a leadership "depth chart."

- *Attend to the bottom half:* Managers in most organizations focus their attention on their top performers and let lesser performers weed themselves out. By comparison, the Marines view a team as being no stronger than its weakest link and devote a great deal of personal attention to building the skills and confidence of people who are struggling.

- *Use discipline to build pride:* The Marines have lots of rules and you have to obey them or you're out. At the same time, however, they refuse to give up on people, and they build teams who self-police their own code of conduct. By the time that recruits weather "the Crucible," a grueling 54-hour combat simulation, they have learned to take pride in working as a team under the most adverse circumstances.

Unlike a corporation, the Marines must keep most of their recruits for a minimum four-year enlistment. Many of them come from underprivileged backgrounds, and lack self-discipline before they join the Corps. Despite these factors—or perhaps because of them—McKinsey found that the Marines far outranked every for-profit organization it studied in creating morale and commitment among their frontline employees.

While many myths surround business culture, some of its stereotypes are also accurate. Firms who pay attention to their cultures tend to be much more employee- and customer-oriented. Cultures that are actively promoted tend to become guiding principles for their parent organizations. And above all, firms who lead their market for a long time—in almost any market—generally have strong cultures. By separating myth from reality, you can begin to take steps to understand and manage the culture of your own workplace. More important, you can start building this culture as a key asset of your long-term business capital.

ASSESSING YOUR OWN WORKPLACE CULTURE

There are all kinds of metrics for the financial side of your business or workplace. There are also good metrics for most aspects of your operations, ranging from productivity to turnover. But culture is a little harder to quantify, even when it plays a dominant role in how successful your other metrics are. At the same time, you can measure some key factors to provide an overall snapshot of your existing culture.

The simple test that follows will provide an overview of the strengths of your own culture. There are two choices for each statement, representing different but equally valid perspectives on workplace values. Choose the statement that applies more accurately to your own environment, and mark the appropriate answer.

1. A. We have a system behind what we do.

B. We take pride in figuring things out as we go along.

ANSWER: _____

2. A. One clear guiding principle drives our daily operations.

B. We make most decisions situationally.

ANSWER: _____

3. A. We primarily measure how well people reach overall quality and service goals.

   B. We primarily measure individual productivity and output.

   ANSWER: _____

4. A. We feel that treating our employees well comes first.

   B. We feel that treating our customers well comes first.

   ANSWER: _____

5. A. Our frontline employees have a great deal of autonomy and authority.

   B. Things work more smoothly when managers approve variations from procedure.

   ANSWER: _____

6. A. We have a wider variety of job titles and responsibilities than similar places.

   B. We don't believe in having too many specialties within our workforce.

   ANSWER: _____

7. A. Our projects often cross departmental boundaries.

   B. We promote a great deal of departmental autonomy.

   ANSWER: _____

8. A. We have a very structured recruiting process with substantial team involvement.

   B. We leave the details of hiring to individual managers.

   ANSWER: _____

9. A. People are primarily evaluated on how well they serve others in the organization.

B. People are primarily evaluated on how well they do their jobs.

ANSWER: _____

10. A. We are willing to bend the rules to react quickly to competition.

B. We are very careful about putting proven processes at risk for the sake of expediency.

ANSWER: _____

11. A. We are ahead of similar firms in our use of technology.

B. We are content to let others make technology mistakes and be "late adopters."

ANSWER: _____

12. A. We spend more time analyzing customer trends than competitors.

B. We spend more time analyzing competitors than customer trends.

ANSWER: _____

13. A. We feel that excellent customer service is primarily a process.

B. We feel that excellent customer service is primarily an attitude.

ANSWER: _____

14. A. We benchmark our processes by being customers ourselves.

B. We rely on customer feedback to benchmark our processes.

ANSWER: _____

15. A. We capture data about customer transactions and react to it strategically.

B. We respond to customer issues as problems arise.

ANSWER: _____

16. A. We foster job-related outside activities.

B. We believe in keeping work-life and outside activities separate.

ANSWER: _____

17. A. We are very active in using our professional talents in the community.

B. Our charitable and community activities are mostly financial in nature.

ANSWER: _____

18. A. We see even the most humble of jobs as professions.

B. We see entry positions as stepping-stones rather than as ends unto themselves.

ANSWER: _____

19. A. We develop most leaders from within.

B. We hire the best leaders we can find, and many come from the outside.

ANSWER: _____

20. A. Our employees are focused on the big picture of our organization.

B. Our employees are focused on their specific jobs.

ANSWER: _____

21. A. Our upper management communicates with all employees at least weekly.

B. Our upper management communicates with all employees as events arise.

ANSWER: _____

To interpret your score, count up the number of A choices you answered, and use the chart on the next page to assess your own specific cultural traits.

If you had two or three A answers for this group of questions:	Then this is a strong cultural trait in your organization:
1–3	Operational excellence
4–6	Positive working environment
7–9	Team building
10–12	Managing growth and change
13–15	Customer service
16–18	Passion for your work
19–21	Visionary leadership

Which of these traits are the most important ones? All of them. But every organization is different, just like every human being is, which means that each has its unique set of cultural traits, and each has factors that are more important to its business environment. This test represents a quick scan of where your culture aligns with the best practices of many of today's leading firms, and where you may find new ideas to learn and grow from. (And if none of these areas score highly for your organization, don't worry, you have plenty of company and some great new things to learn.) Each of these areas is discussed in chapter-length detail in the rest of the book, so read on and see how other workplaces from all walks of life have built their own success around these core business culture traits.

2

The Strategists
Driving Operational Excellence

Strategists are people who look far beyond the individual transactions of daily work life and see systems that drive their long-term success. While most people concentrate on the myriad details of what they do, Strategists look for the one unifying value that defines who they are and, in the process, provides direction for all the other details that follow. Strategists can be described in terms of three core principles:

1. We have a system behind what we do. If you were delivering a package overnight 100 miles away, would you fly it to Memphis first? By developing a hub-and-spoke delivery system with near flawless tracking capabilities, FedEx developed a system that reliably moves hundreds of thousands of packages overnight, around a system that makes Memphis International Airport one of the world's busiest between 2 and 4 AM—and has since scaled to numerous other hubs.

2. One clear guiding principle drives our daily operations. When Dell Computer was first begun in a college dorm room, for example, it survived by selling directly to customers from orders already in hand. Today, the same principle drives a $30-billion-per-year operation that is now the world's largest computer manufacturer.

3. We primarily measure how well people reach overall quality and service goals. Many companies constantly measure how productive their employees are, often breeding compliance rather than excellence. But at Continental Airlines, people are rewarded financially for the success of the end product itself—on-time arrivals. This bonus has been paid nearly every month since the program was instituted—and the cost of this incentive is far outweighed by the savings of not running late.

In a sense, Strategists can be described in terms of their corporate slogans: "Absolutely, positively overnight." "Guaranteed to be there." "Engineered like no other car in the world." These tag lines for FedEx, Blockbuster, and Mercedes Benz send very public messages that define these companies in terms of the one core value that drives their operations. A subtler but equally important point is that these values play an important role in defining their workplace cultures as well. For many organizations, the quest to become the best at one specific thing has effects that go far beyond the thing itself, and ultimately paves the road to a best-of-class organization.

Striving for excellence has an impact that goes far beyond the goals of a team, into cultural values that can infect every other area of an organization. If you work in the finance department of a top-rated airline, for example, your workplace culture is probably much different from that of a poorly rated airline—even if you never set foot near an airplane. More important, the road to workplace success may begin as simply as committing to perform just one thing better than anyone else. Here, we will look at the process by which "execution" goes beyond performance and becomes your internal values.

HOW SYSTEMS DEFINE YOUR CULTURE

Every workplace has its basic operating procedures. For many organizations, these procedures can become a collection of soulless rules and policies. But for Strategists, they are a microcosm of their cultural values, which, in turn, make them successful. Let's look at a firm that changed the whole way many of us purchase eyewear.

LENSCRAFTERS: A System That Drove a Culture

Once upon a time, most people waited weeks to get a new pair of eyeglasses. First, you made an appointment to see your eye doctor. Afterwards, you visited an optician to select a pair of frames. Your prescription then would be sent to a lab, the glasses were made, and then they were sent back to your friendly optician. In 1983, a company named **LensCrafters** had the bright idea to move both the optical lab and the eye doctors into the store itself, and make the eyeglasses on demand. Suddenly, you could decide to have your eyes checked while eating lunch at the mall, and return to work shortly afterward wearing a new pair of glasses.

Today, nearly 20 years later, LensCrafters is the largest optical retailer in the world—and, as of this writing, one of the top 100 employers to work for in *Fortune* magazine's annual survey, enjoying one of the lowest turnover rates of *any* major retail chain. And it continues to post some of the highest levels of revenue and profits in its history, in what now has become a billion-dollar-plus annual operation with nearly 1,000 retail outlets and 18,000 employees throughout North America.

We tend to think of business culture as a soft skill, separate from your business operations. In reality, these operations often define your culture, rather than the other way around. How you execute your business inexorably becomes a philosophy, and this philosophy then creates values that drive your personal relationships, your service quality, and your daily business decisions. In this sense, business culture invariably follows Friedrich Nietzsche's dictum "to be is to do."

Let's take LensCrafters as a case in point. Does it succeed today because it makes eyeglasses in about an hour? No, almost every one of its major competitors now does the same thing. But when the company decided to break the mold of its industry, its decision created side effects throughout the rest of its operations, and, in turn, throughout its culture. These side effects created a business environment that its competitors found difficult to duplicate. Here are some of the things necessary to become the first business to deliver eyeglasses in an hour, and where they might lead:

Delivering eyeglasses in an hour requires:
↓
A coordinated team effort,
which requires
↓
A motivated workforce,
which requires
↓
A positive workplace and opportunities for personal growth,
which creates
↓
Excellent service,
which results in
↓
Customer focus,
which drives
↓
Hours, policies, store locations, and other business decisions.

So, as you follow this to its logical conclusion, the path towards a seemingly straightforward business goal brings along a great many workplace values in its wake. And in time, these values often overtake the operations themselves. When LensCrafters first started nearly two decades ago, its advertising slogan was the obvious "Glasses in about an hour." Later, it evolved to become "Helping the world to see better, one person at a time," which, not coincidentally, remains its mission statement. Ultimately, we come full circle to find the place where LensCrafters started—its operations—creating a culture that, in turn, leads its operations into the future.

Becoming the very best at something—at anything—is one of the most powerful motivating values in any organization. A core value of operating excellence goes far beyond the operations themselves and becomes a microcosm of the teamwork, innovation, benchmarking, and other values needed to create it. For one electronics retailer, this philosophy has succeeded in taking it to the top of a very competitive industry.

BEST BUY: Execution Breeds Culture

Most people think that being customer-centric means providing good service quality. But at electronics giant **Best Buy,** this goes far beyond employing friendly people, into a passion for logistics. "Getting close to the customer" means having one of the most sophisticated inventory management systems in the retail industry, investing heavily in software tools to understand customer buying habits in real time, and even creating a master parts catalog of components used in the products it sells to speed repair times. In the process, the company has grown to be America's largest consumer electronics retailer, with more than 400 stores and $15 billion in annual revenues.

In the case of Best Buy, having strong systems behind its distribution, pricing, and product service models also encourages its workplace culture, where strong customer service and knowledgeable, noncommisioned floor staff have helped fuel its massive growth over the past decade. Unfortunately, the converse is true as well—poor execution often creates a poor culture. In workplaces where people are hamstrung from doing a good job by poor processes, it is not unusual to find employee disinterest, low morale, and dysfunctional management as well—as evidenced by the experiences one Western newspaper had with its telephone company.

THE TELECOMMUNICATIONS FIRM THAT COULDN'T COMMUNICATE

When a Montana newspaper disputed a bill from its local telephone company, following a botched telephone system installation, it had no idea that it would be embarking on nearly a yearlong odyssey. First, the editor tried to send a complaint letter to the company, but its customer-service department told him that there was no place to send it, suggesting that he instead try the company Web site. Finding no place for complaints online either, he finally pasted his message into a comment form. Three days later, he was informed that someone would follow up with him on his complaint, which never happened.

Eventually the editor reached a company representative by telephone and the company informed him that the newspaper's service would not be disconnected while the amount was in dispute. The newspaper, however, continued to receive disconnection notices for several months. Finally, its service was disconnected one day, and when the newspaper called about this, it discovered that the company had, in fact, resolved the dispute in the newspaper's favor some time ago, but never bothered to notify either the newspaper or its own billing department. Nonetheless, the newspaper was informed that between 24 and 48 hours would be needed to restore service. When the editor told its customer-service representative, "You guys are the worst company on earth," the representative agreed with him. Shortly afterwards, the newspaper switched its $12,000-per-year account to another service provider.

Dysfunctional operations can quickly affect an entire company, or even an entire industry. According to the Federal Communications Commission, for example, overall consumer dissatisfaction with telephone services rose by more than 50 percent between 1997 and 2000, and the number of complaints per customer has more than tripled in the past decade. Behind numbers like these are both a global cost in revenue and market share, and a more human cost in morale and turnover. No one wants to come home from work saying, "I work for the worst company in the business," and this death spiral eventually infects employee quality and customer confidence.

THREE FACTORS BEHIND A STRATEGIST

So, what traits do Strategists possess? If you look critically at Strategists' companies that succeed because of a culture led by their operations, you will often find three factors at work.

A Sharp Focus on Being the Best

For most companies, regardless of what they may say publicly, the natural order seems to be one of being "good enough" in several areas. By comparison, Strategists break the mold by picking one thing and doing it better than anyone else. When one firm decided to apply this philosophy to the humble doughnut, it created one of the most profitable fast-food franchises in history.

KRISPY KREME: Seeking Perfection in a Glazed Doughnut

Krispy Kreme became famous for producing one thing very well—hot, glazed doughnuts. Outside each store, a large neon sign lights up when its glazed doughnuts are hot and fresh from the oven, and it is not unusual to see lines of cars spilling out into the street when the "hot" light is on. Inside each store is a glass wall that is placed alongside a spotless assembly line where dough is perfectly formed, fried for just the right length of time, and transported through a viscous waterfall of sweet glaze. Signs describe the process in detail, as you wait to pick up your own fresh doughnuts at the end of the line. In an interview with *Fast Company* magazine, Krispy Kreme's "minister of culture" Mike

Cecil noted, "To our customers, Krispy Kremes are more than doughnuts, they're stories. People get a dreamy look in their eyes when they talk about them."

Started in 1937, and long an institution in the southern United States, Krispy Kreme has witnessed an unparalleled growth surge in recent years. In the past year alone, it has grown nearly 40 percent to exceed a half billion dollars in annual revenue. But growth in stores has never translated to diversification in menu items. Go to a Krispy Kreme store, and you will find doughnuts, coffee, and soft drinks, period. This simple menu continues to draw huge crowds and critical acclaim because, according to noted southern-born writer and humorist Roy Blount, Jr., "They are to other doughnuts what angels are to people."

You cannot underestimate the power of focusing on one thing, and doing it better than anyone else. One evening, I drove by a Krispy Kreme store in Buffalo, New York, and noticed cars extending around the block. I returned later in the wee hours of the morning and still had to wait more than half an hour to reach the drive-through window. For a store that had already been open for nearly three months, on a thoroughfare crowded with other chain doughnut stores, the quest to create the very best doughnut seemed to literally create magic—and revenues—out of thin air.

A System That Works

Most Strategist cultures don't make up the rules as they go along. They define a system that institutionalizes their level of performance, and these systems ultimately define their core values as well. For example, The Boatyard Grill, the upstate New York restaurant discussed in Chapter 1, views customer service as a structured process of managing the guest experience, in an industry where many restaurants see service as just another quickly forgotten training program. According to owner Mark Campagnolo, "For us, it's a philosophy and not just a focus. We base our operations around five fundamentals:

1. Guest recognition: Assist and acknowledge anyone within a five-foot radius.
2. Customer kindness: Be courteous, concerned, and friendly at all times, regardless of the circumstance.
3. Anticipate and respond: Be on the lookout for body language and tone of voice, and then handle situations professionally. When needed, practice service recovery based on our "baker's dozen fix" (make it right, then give something extra), and remember that the customer is not always right, but he or she is always the customer.
4. Make it memorable: We only have a few seconds to make a lasting impression.
5. Focus on people: It's people, not interiors, furniture, or fixtures, that have made us successful over the years.

These five fundamentals are more than just pages from a training manual. Mark and his managers are constantly on the floor, measuring how well people execute, and coaching them in real time on the Boatyard way. As a result, it is not unusual for Boatyard personnel to help customers to their cars, prepare special orders, or remember their regulars. According to Mark, the system drives the philosophy, rather than the other way around. "We have to start with the basic understanding that we want to build loyalty and not check averages. We shift the focus of profitability by building loyal customers, building loyal employees, and *then* building revenues by doing the first two things."

Quantum Levels of Improvement

If one factor differentiates Strategists from others, it is that strong cultures are often built around operations that broke the mold of their business. Southwest Airlines profitably offers low-fare, point-to-point service by getting more trips per day out of their planes than other carriers, driven by a near fanatical devotion to teamwork. Wendy's prepares hamburgers to order in real time, so that every order is a "special order." And Dell Computer leverages the Internet as its primary sales and customer-service channel. In the process, each of them has defined a business culture that is far different from most of their competitors.

Average companies benchmark their competition and try to improve on what they do. As logical as that may seem, there is now a growing body of opinion that competitive analysis is a bad foundation for a business, as it may lead to a mind-set of incremental improvement. Take a consumer product such as a VCR, for example. Over time, companies have added features and functions to VCRs, to the point where people must often be like computer programmers to use them. In a similar manner, many organizations look at their business processes and try to be a little better than everyone else. By comparison, the cultures of dominant firms often started by thinking far outside of that box.

Here, we should draw a sharp distinction between product innovation and business culture. It is your operations, and not your products and services, that define who you are and what your culture is. Products may be what you sell, but your operations define what you do—and ultimately, in many cases, who you are. If you develop a hot-selling new appliance, it may have no impact whatsoever on cultural factors such as morale, turnover, service quality, or long-term viability. However, if you develop a new team approach to building an appliance, you have the potential to change the culture of your workplace, which, in turn, may drive your long-term success.

Ultimately, lessons—often unspoken—are hiding within your daily business operations. By listening carefully to these lessons, you may develop an entirely new perspective about your business's relationship to employees and customers. More important, they give you the power to define what you want your workplace to be, now and in the future. For many organizations, their core values are not soft skills or ethereal boardroom concepts, but the reality of what is happening every day on the shop floor or at the planning table. Understand them, and you can harness these operations to support the culture that you envision for the future.

ENSURING SUCCESS BY MEASURING IT—THE RIGHT WAY

The best firms are not successful because they think that they are. They know that they are, because they measure it—and a key point of being a Strategist is having measures that tell you that your systems are working. A company like FedEx, for instance, knows precisely where your package is at any given time through a process of scanning your package as it goes through each stage of the delivery cycle. This not only allows you to track the exact status of your delivery, but also provides FedEx itself with a gold mine of statistics about its package delivery operations.

At the same time, Strategists have a key advantage over other people who track performance: they focus on the end results, rather than micromanaging the steps that get you there. So rather than focusing on how many bolts get tightened by each person on the assembly line—and getting people to sullenly tighten more—they focus on how many cars are being built each day, and get people excited about working as a team to improve performance. For most organizations, the whole area of performance measurement is fraught with peril, and it would not be an overstatement to say that more dysfunctional cultures are created by poor metrics than by any other factor. And Strategists understand that following simple human nature has a paradoxical effect when it comes to metrics: measuring performance can cause it to decline, productivity benchmarks can lower productivity, and rewards can destroy motivation. Here is how your organization can sidestep the perils of bad metrics and still keep track of your operations.

If there ever was an example of where a good workplace culture collides head-on with human nature, it is in the area of performance measurement. Managers are in the business of delivering results, and many of them feel that this means continually measuring employee performance—both to make sure that they meet the standards of their jobs and to "motivate" them to perform better. In many cases, this belief all but guarantees mediocre performance and poor motivation. Let's look at one example of the wrong kind of focus on productivity from the call center profession.

BE CAREFUL WHAT YOU MEASURE

What happens when you measure agents in a call center on the seemingly obvious statistic of how many calls they handle per hour? Often, the answer is short calls and poor service quality. Help desk author and consultant Char LaBounty once described how agents in one call center would arrange for friends to call them several times a day to keep their numbers up, or simply hang up "accidentally" on people to get to the next call quicker. Those customers who did get through often found themselves pushed off the phone with indelicate haste, whether their issues were resolved satisfactorily or not.

Suppose we take it a step further and start measuring instead how many customers' problems get resolved on the first call? According to LaBounty, another call center responded by considering a referral to another person as a "resolution," so that if the call could be passed immediately to someone else, the problem was solved. This meant that many problems that could have been solved by one person were now being passed to several people for the sake of statistics. Ironically, this team had already won a company award for improving its resolution rate by the time their improvement technique surfaced.

And it gets worse from there—in some cases, much worse. Some of the stories other call center professionals have shared include:

- Technicians asking customers to erase their hard drives—costing the customer hours of reloading their software—rather than taking the time to diagnose a problem
- Technicians masquerading as supervisors for each other, to prevent themselves from getting "dinged" when a customer asked to speak to a real supervisor.
- Support centers fixing defective computers with parts from other defective computers—and then shipping them out with minimal testing to keep their productivity numbers up.

There is a law of unintended consequences at work in situations like these. Rewards for seemingly good things such as productivity and profitability have the paradoxical effect of ruining the very things they were designed to improve, because the metrics soon take precedence over the values behind them. For example, when a major computer manufacturer once tried to get its call center reps to spend no more than 13 minutes on the phone with customers as an efficiency measure, and cut off monthly bonuses for transgressors, the results were predictable. People did whatever they could to get customers off the phone, customer satisfaction plummeted, referral business dropped from 50 percent to 30 percent, and the policy was soon scrapped. Without the right underlying values, human nature ultimately governs situations like these, and human nature inevitably seeks short-term gains at the expense of more important long-term goals.

The irony is that successful Strategist cultures have shown that you can have your cake and eat it, too. It is eminently possible to have good workplace metrics, without disenfranchising your workplace or your customers. Some of the values that transcend this human nature and drive truly successful performance evaluation include the following:

Measuring versus Monitoring

Looking at the call center examples previously mentioned, the results they are ultimately seeking are happy customers. But paradoxically, using productivity measures to reward and punish employees in these situations all but guarantees fewer happy customers. Moreover, this problem has become endemic to their industry—computer technical support has become one of the lowest-rated services in consumer history, according to a 1990s survey by *Consumer Reports*.

Still, isn't a lack of performance measurement a little like a university without grades, or tennis without a net? If you don't measure how well you are doing, aren't you doomed to people doing as little as possible? The way out of this quandary lies in understanding the difference between primary goals and secondary goals:

- *Primary goals* are the things your organization ultimately wants, such as profitability, customer satisfaction, market share, and quality.
- *Secondary goals* are the factors that help you reach your primary goals, such as productivity, response time, efficiency, and reject rates.

Primary goals are the only ones that matter to your customers. No one patronizes your business because of your productivity, and no customer will ever get upset because of how much material you waste on the shop floor. But customers care a great deal about getting a quality product and experiencing good service. All they want, and all your upper management wants, are these primary results. This simple fact drives a golden rule of good workplace metrics:

Measure primary goals and _monitor_ secondary goals.

What is the difference between measuring and monitoring? The two terms have a subtle distinction that makes all the difference in the world.

Measuring is conducted publicly, for all the team to see. If your customer satisfaction levels are up or down, each employee should know about it. For example, hardware giant Lowe's announces its stock price daily over the public-address system of its stores. Their employees, most of whom are also stockholders, have a direct stake in the ups and downs of this stock price. There is never a downside to employees knowing the status of a company's primary goals.

Monitoring, on the other hand, is generally performed in private, in much the same way that security personnel monitor remote cameras at a store. Monitoring ongoing metrics such as personal productivity allows managers to intervene only when people vary far from the norms. It provides a mechanism to deal with individual performance problems, without making other employees feel like caged chickens whose every move is watched. These statistics then become trends to study for overall improvement, rather than a yoke around the individual. The vast majority of people thus carry on with their jobs and feel that they are doing fine, as things should be. More important, these statistics yield clues for how you might improve everyone's productivity, with the involvement of the team itself.

When you monitor instead of measure, you take the peer pressure element out of individual performance metrics. Confronting people with their own performance metrics, however well intentioned it may be, will inevitably cause them to put your metrics ahead of the interests of the customer or the company. Even worse, they can lead to tacit group pressure to lower your performance bar. As one former aerospace worker puts it, "We never liked people who worked hard, because they made it difficult for everyone else. Getting along with everyone in our department meant keeping the work pace slow and steady." One European firm's employees went so far as to sue a group of visiting Japanese workers—successfully!—because they were working too fast and making the rest of them look bad.

Being Careful What You Reward

The right kinds of rewards and the right kind of recognition are critical to reinforcing the importance of each person in your organization. These include rewards for a job well done, recognition of milestones, and using performance reviews as a means to encourage and motivate people about their strengths, among other measures. Putting a culture of rewards and recognition into play not only demonstrates the level of respect that you have for your team members but also often has a tangible impact on your bottom line.

At the same time, rewards can lose their impact when they become a tool to control rather than motivate people. Many people who lead organizations unknowingly have a deterministic view of performance—they see rewards and punishments as levers that control the results they will get. In reality, the opposite is often true. Employees who are rewarded for productivity alone often skimp on product or service quality, in much the same way that executives who are rewarded for high stock prices can allow situations like we have seen as of this writing at companies like Enron and WorldCom. Conversely, a team who is given the responsibility and autonomy to improve productivity, and then rewarded when they deliver appropriate results, is much less likely to simply "game the system" just to get rewarded.

Psychologist Edward Deci conducted a controversial study in the 1970s, showing that most rewards actually destroy people's intrinsic motivation—and three decades later, many subsequent studies have corroborated his findings. In one early experiment, he paid one group of children to solve puzzles, while another group was unpaid. He found that the former group stopped solving the puzzles as soon as the reward stopped, while the latter group continued on. Expanding these results to the workplace, other studies have shown that moving from a piecework compensation structure (where you are paid according to your output) to a straight salary resulted in no change whatsoever in productivity.

Piecework itself is an ideal microcosm of the downside of performance measurement. The simple and seemingly obvious idea that people should be paid according to their productivity can play a major role in contentious labor relations. According to legendary quality expert W. Edwards Deming, "Piecework is man's lowest degradation." First and foremost, the piecework model leads to the same conflict between quantity and quality that was discussed previously with call centers. Given a choice between doing a job right and doing a shoddy job with higher productivity, most will vote with their wallets and do the latter. Moreover, setting a piecework rate itself can quickly become an impediment to productivity:

- If the rate is too high, morale suffers.
- If the rate is too low, production suffers.
- Even if the rate is just right, there is a natural disincentive to raise the performance bar in the future.

Suppose that one morning, someone has a brilliant idea for rearranging your work flow, and you now can suddenly produce twice as much of your product. Cause for celebration? In a piecework environment, such a move is more likely to start a war. Employees will resist raising the permanent standards by that much, managers will equally resist raising everyone's hourly compensation by that much, and what should have been a great thing instead becomes a tug-of-war. And ultimately, what your organization wants—higher output—becomes the thing that everyone on the front lines secretly doesn't want.

Also, a much deeper issue goes far beyond individual performance and compensation: do people collaborate or compete? A recent Towers Perrin study found that most corporate reward plans inhibit firms from moving away from a hierarchical business structure towards a greater amount of teamwork. Moving into the trenches, most employees are hard-pressed to collaborate with others if it affects their performance appraisal, or the size of their paycheck. And the wrong rewards can easily backfire. For example, consultant Milton Zall tells of one engineering firm that rewarded its employees for designing projects under budget—and one engineer earned his reward by simply making each floor of the building six inches shorter. He saved the company money, but he did so by taking something away from the customer. And when this behavior is taken to the limit, the balance between employee incentives and buildings where tall people have to duck their heads ultimately becomes very murky.

Industry-wide, the cultural dilemma of pay-for-performance is widespread. According to one study, nearly 75 percent of firms have some type of variable compensation plan, yet less than half of the companies surveyed felt that they met key business objectives. So, if productivity incentives such as piecework represent a poor strategy, how should you reward your employees? According to business performance expert Alfie Kohn, the best strategy is to "pay workers well and fairly and then do everything possible to help them forget about money." Rewards still have their place in the eyes of many workplaces, but there is an important difference between sharing profits or compensating a superlative effort versus constantly putting a carrot in front of the horse as a productivity tool. Put another way, the ideal reward strategy should move away from workplace metrics (like piece-rate bonuses) and move towards workplace values (like collaborative effort towards common goals).

Fostering an Environment of Team Performance Improvement

The crowning irony of performance measurement is that when you cease standing behind people with a stopwatch, and stop rewarding people for productivity metrics, you create an environment that removes many of the roadblocks to quantum increases in productivity. With no peer pressure and high levels of personal authority, employees become partners in the goals of your organization, rather than slaves to the metrics of it.

When you trust your team to meet larger goals, and give them the authority to make it happen, there is often no limit on what they can accomplish. One General Electric facility in Puerto Rico, for example, has committees on improving company operations that are run by hourly employees—and managers only attend these meetings at the specific request of the teams. Since implementing this approach, productivity has improved by 20 percent.

Over a decade ago, one of the great business buzzwords was *empowerment,* which describes an ideal by which people had the authority and responsibility to take ownership of their workplace destiny. Like many other buzzwords, it eventually took its bumps and bruises in the real world, as it became a code word for everything from workplace anarchy to simple over-work (as in, "we'll empower you to figure out how to do twice as much work with half as many resources"). Yet underneath it all is the germ of a very important and enduring concept of business culture: the more author-ity you can put in the lowest levels of your team, the more ownership they will take to improve their own workplace performance. When employees feel like owners, they will strive for the organization's greater good in a way that traditional rewards and punishments will never accomplish.

HOW TECHNOLOGY HELPS THE STRATEGIST AND HURTS OTHERS

The cultural divide between good metrics and bad ones is likely to grow nothing but greater over the years, because of fundamental trends in business processes and technology. For example, CRM, an acronym for Customer Relationship Management, represents a multibillion-dollar-a-year industry that provides tools to measure almost every aspect of your customer interactions—how often they contact you, what they buy, what questions or problems they have, and much more. This data can be tremen-dously powerful within the right cultural context. Strategists can use CRM data, for instance, to determine how many people eat fish at their restaurant on weekends, how many green widgets to manufacture versus blue ones, or where to build their next hotel. More important, it helps them get closer to their customers, and to look critically at their business processes as they re-late to customer satisfaction.

Trends such as these represent a tremendous opportunity for the Strate-gist. By having a "dashboard" of information from sources such as CRM and other operations, it is now possible to keep your finger on the pulse of an organization in real time—and see the impact of changes to your system in real time as well. This allows Strategist cultures to build systems that provide better feedback, so that the operations and the culture can learn from each other faster than ever before. A restaurant, for example, can con-tinually fine-tune its menu to suit customer preferences, a customer-service center can see trends in what makes their customers unhappy, and businesses of all sizes can seek fundamental ways to improve their operations based on real-time feedback and analysis.

At the same time, for those who aren't Strategists, trends like using CRM have created an era where it is now easier than ever to micromeasure every little facet of productivity. One telephone company employee, for instance, noted that the employees were monitored and measured for how much "upselling" they do when customers call in for service, even when he personally felt it was inappropriate. ("Hello, Mrs. Smith, I'm sorry to hear that your house was destroyed in a hurricane. Could we interest you in purchasing call waiting?") Here, a very good metric (overall sales volume) has been replaced by a more precise but very bad metric (e.g., what must be said to each customer), because the tools now exist to monitor the latter. This, in turn, becomes part of what defines your workplace culture.

At a deeper level, this phenomenon also helps explain why some people invest six-figure sums to improve their customer-service operations and make them much better, while others spend the same amount and make them much worse. It is the implementation of this technology—or rather, the culture in which the technology is implemented—that causes it to behave as swords or as plowshares. At a deeper level, technology has become a magnifying glass for workplace culture, and we now live in a world where the rich get richer and the poor get poorer faster than ever. This fact represents a significant competitive advantage for the Strategist, who realizes that cultural values—and not short-term business processes—form the ideal basis for most performance metrics.

"SUGGESTION BOX" WORKPLACES VERSUS HIGH-PERFORMANCE CULTURES

The difference between workplaces where people complain and ones where people perform is often the degree of responsibility and authority found at the workplace level. Strategists combine good systems with putting as much authority at the team level as possible. A theme park employee, for example, may have clear guidelines for being "in character," and a chain restaurant manager may have strong standards for the restaurant's food and service. But when either is combined with the autonomy to managing their customer and employee experience, the result is a level of quality you will never find in an "I just work here" culture. In recent years, one restaurant chain put these concepts into practice to create one of the fastest-growing full-service eateries of all time.

OUTBACK STEAKHOUSE: "No Rules," But Strong Procedures

Visit any Outback Steakhouse and you will find the restaurant manager's name painted over the door with the title of "proprietor." This is more than just a polite turn of phrase. When Outback began its operations, the company helped finance its growth by requiring managers to invest some of their own funds and take a partial ownership position in their restaurants.

The side effects of this move were as much cultural as financial. Outback Steakhouse is remarkably consistent in its quality and service experience, thanks to the involvement of individual restaurant managers, and this, in turn, helped fuel the chain's status as the hottest growth restaurant of the late 1990s. According to one Outback manager, "We are always looking to improve ourselves by paying attention to details and consistently meeting and exceeding our own standards. Our managers make a commitment to our customers to deliver quality food and concentrated service in a friendly atmosphere. For example, we have a management-level person inspecting the plated food as it comes out of the kitchen, instead of an hourly employee, enabling me to personally oversee almost every aspect of the overall guest experience."

This culture of ownership has a global aspect as well. When you go to Outback's Web site to find out about franchising one of its restaurants, you will find a surprising message behind their "Franchise Information" link—you can't. Apart from some early franchise operations, the chain's restaurants are largely company-owned, and they plan to keep it that way as they grow into the future.

Sadly, this sense of personal responsibility is still lacking in many workplace cultures. How many times do you go to a retail store and see sales clerks gossiping with each other, and ignoring you as you wait for service? Or dissing their employer in front of you? Or even yakking openly on a cell phone with their boyfriend? For most of us, situations like this happen more often than we care to remember. At a deeper level, situations like these are a symptom of one of the biggest values impeding workplace quality—a lack of ownership.

TELL BUCKY ABOUT IT

One afternoon I went to a customer-service counter of a large discount store, asking for help to find something. The woman behind the counter didn't acknowledge me or make eye contact, but simply picked up the phone and drawled, "Bucky, call line five," before burying her face in paperwork again. After a few minutes of waiting silently, I finally asked if anyone else could help, and again the response was "Bucky, line five." She never even looked up again, and it became clear after a while that getting help was Bucky's problem and not hers. After several more minutes, I left and bought what I was looking for at another store.

Not surprisingly, this store's parent chain is not doing well financially, and business analysts have pointed to many economic and competitive factors as reasons. But when you get down to the real reasons that people don't shop there, they should put down their annual reports and talk to Bucky. There are underlying cultural factors that cause people in this store to hate their jobs and see customers as a bother, and no amount of debenture financing will change them.

Ownership is not simply a good or bad trait. It is rather a continuum that goes from one bad extreme to another, with an optimal point squarely in the middle. At one end, you guard the interests of your employer (or yourself), and at the other, you guard the interests of your customer. In between these two points lies an enlightened self-interest in both sides of the transaction. Let's say, for example, that you work in a cafeteria and a customer is complaining about the food. Here are the points on the continuum:

- *Too much employer focus:* "There's nothing wrong with the food. I ate it, and it's fine."
- *Too much customer focus:* "I agree, the food really does stink here."
- *The happy midpoint:* "We want you to have a good meal here. What can we do to make this right?"

Surprisingly, this concept of ownership doesn't correlate well with actual ownership. The old saw of "treat customers as though your name was on the door" sounds good in theory, but in reality, many small businesses provide poor service to their customers, and a surprising number of entry-level store clerks provide excellent service. Ownership is a deeper cultural concept that ultimately relates to each employee's relationship with his or her job. Cultures who foster it harness the power of their team's energy and innovation, rather than simple forced labor, and leverage it as a strategic competitive asset.

TURNING OPERATIONAL GOALS INTO CULTURAL GOALS

If you were to read the mission statements and vision statements for businesses of any size, you would be hard-pressed to find one that doesn't involve a commitment to be the best in its profession. And yet, a clear gap exists between these claims and the reality of most workplaces. This is because deeper values drive a culture of excellence. Telling everyone to work harder will not produce it, but a realistic game plan to become the best in their profession will. Such a game plan, driven by the right values, is perhaps the most powerful cultural change agent possible.

Once again, the split between human nature and core values remains at the heart of most business operations. If your company makes widgets, human nature tells you to take seemingly obvious steps like rewarding productivity, creating rules and policies designed to guard against inefficiency, and benchmarking yourself against your competitors. But when you take a different path and invest in people, grant authority, set high standards, and innovate, the equation changes dramatically for the better. If you look closely at the operations of the Strategists versus traditional business wisdom, you will often find that the long way around is the shortest way home.

This means that the path to developing a Strategist culture starts with taking a fresh look at your operations. Success is often as simple as choosing to become the very best at one specific thing, and letting the values that drive this become your new business practices. More than any area of your workplace, your daily operations represent a tangible, measurable place to replace human nature with the values of excellence, and see where these values take you.

The Vanguard Group
How Index Funds Drive a Culture

Many firms have a product that goes far beyond simply being what they sell, and becomes a metaphor for the culture of the company itself. In the case of investment giant The Vanguard Group, that product is the index fund. These funds not only represent the investment vehicle of choice for a majority of its $580 billion in assets, but in many ways serve as a defining value for Vanguard itself.

The index fund is a deceptively simple concept. Developed by Vanguard founder John Bogle in the mid-1970s, these funds invest proportionately in each of the stocks that compose a market index, such as the Standard & Poor's 500, so that the performance of the fund is, by definition, tied to the performance of the index. The difference? Index funds can essentially be managed on autopilot, using computers instead of expensive fund managers. This helps drive the incredibly low fee structure of Vanguard funds: an index fund may have as little as one-eighth the fees of a similar managed fund. More important, index funds have proven to be very sound investment vehicles, which often outperform the mutual fund market as a whole. Nearly two-thirds of Vanguard's assets are now held by index funds in stocks, bonds, and other investment vehicles. And at a deeper level, this strategy drives a culture that revolves around creating sound investment choices with the lowest-possible fees.

This system fuels Vanguard's public image in the marketplace as a no-frills, low-cost philosophy of investing. In pioneering the concept of the index fund, it created what is now the largest mutual fund in history—the Vanguard 500 Index Fund—and helped open up mutual fund investing to a mass market. More important, its investment philosophy has spawned a unique corporate culture marked by a fanatical devotion to cost control, while still being known for caring management, high job security, and the industry's top customer service ratings.

It almost seems paradoxical to have a company with very low management costs, yet highly committed employees. But its 11,000 employees, known as "crew members" (the last four digits of its toll-free number even spell CREW) work in an environment that respects individuals and eschews layoffs. And as a guiding principle, it constantly seeks to maximize the efficiency of the funds, whose customers, in fact, own the company as fund shareholders. Because the funds themselves own the company, rather than the other way around, Vanguard's financial goals are substantially different from those of an investor-owned firm. Rather than trying to profit from fees that it earns on its investment activity, its overarching goal is to manage its assets at the lowest cost possible.

As the second largest investment firm in the industry, Vanguard is now home to more than 14 million investors—and yet most people have never seen any advertising for the firm. In a corporation that prides itself on diverting as few of its shareholders' assets as possible, this dichotomy is central to who it is. Vanguard is proud of the fact that you will never see the Vanguard golf tournament or Vanguard.com Stadium, and its marketing budget is a tiny fraction of those of other investment firms. And while other investment firms have publicly known star traders, Vanguard takes pride in its low profile, preferring to let the performance of its funds do the talking.

One Vanguard representative recently addressed a large gathering of employees at a client company, and asked them for a show of hands: "How many of you have ever called our toll-free customer-service number?"

About half of the hands go up. "Now, how many of you have ever had to wait on hold?" Nobody raises their hands. He went on to say, "That's part of what makes Vanguard different from other companies. We don't have offices in cities all over the United States. Instead, we put our money into a small number of customer-service centers, and make them the very best that they can be." And indeed, Vanguard's call centers are staffed with very polite, knowledgeable people who are experts in their company's products and services. The Internet fits in well with the company's low-cost fund management strategy as well, and Vanguard's Web site has won numerous awards for its ease-of-use in managing a portfolio online.

Today, Vanguard has evolved to be much more than a group of index funds. In keeping with trends in the financial-services industry, it now offers a full range of investment services, from term life insurance to an online brokerage. Its funds stack up well in industry performance surveys, and its customer-service ratings continue to dominate the industry. Above all, its cost structure remains less than a quarter of the industry average. This cost advantage, and Vanguard's unique cultural values, both still owe a great deal to John Bogle's original vision for a simple investment fund that follows the market with as little fanfare as possible.

3

The Motivators
Creating a Positive Working Environment

Motivators are people who understand that no matter what their business processes are, their success revolves around the commitment of their people. By creating a core value of treating people well, a Motivator knows that his or her own team will ultimately lead the charge to accomplish everything else that the organization needs to thrive. You can break down the Motivators' success into a few key factors:

We feel that treating our employees well comes first. For example, Southwest Airlines has a saying that "the customer comes second"—and it values its own team to the extent that it even capitalizes the word Employee in its written correspondence. This, in turn, has created a work environment that breeds some of the highest customer-satisfaction ratings in the airline industry, year in and year out.

Our frontline employees have a great deal of autonomy and authority. At Nordstrom, you will rarely if ever hear someone say, "I need my manager to approve this." The latitude that its associates have to resolve customer problems is legendary, with stories of employees even going to competing stores to buy replacement products to resolve a customer issue. Over the past century, this philosophy has helped Nordstrom grow from a small Seattle shoe store to a major national clothing retailer, with revenues in excess of $5 billion per year.

We have a wider variety of job titles and responsibilities than do similar places. Visit a Wegmans supermarket and you'll notice an amazing thing: there seems to be more responsibilities and titles in this single grocery store than in a Fortune 500 company. Job responsibilities range from department supervisors to "Strive for 5" coordinators, who run in-store programs teaching shoppers how to get more fruits and vegetables into their daily diets. Not coincidentally, they enjoy long job tenures and low turnover relative to the retail grocery business, and have been a fixture for years on *Fortune* magazine's ranking of the 100 best employers in the United States.

When experts talk about the global competitiveness of specific businesses, the first things they often look at are business processes and balance sheets. But they would do well to first pay attention to the employees in the trenches. Compare the market performance of firms where people "just work here" with ones where there is strong mutual respect within the organization, and you will find that these factors all correlate. There is a stronger connection than most people realize between the front line and the bottom line.

For all the investments that one can make in its business infrastructure, perhaps the most important one is an intangible that never shows up on a balance sheet: a positive working environment. And one of the greatest secrets of the workplace is that the traits that drive one—like respect, autonomy, and personal growth—are not simply attitudes, but cultural values. Few dysfunctional workplaces are simply caused by mean or uncaring people. Rather, they are the result of well-meaning business decisions that slowly chip away at trust, freedom, and autonomy until there is eventually a silent, underlying culture of disrespect. Success in the workplace requires a conscious effort to transcend this path of least resistance.

Motivators whose values create a positive working environment tap in to a source of energy, creativity, and productivity that most firms never experience. It happens when the human nature of command-and-control management is replaced by authority and autonomy on the front lines. It happens when respect for the individual drives employee-friendly policies. It happens when companies encourage and support people's lives and accomplishments outside of work. Above all, it happens when organizations treat their team members as their most valuable internal customers.

RESPECT ISN'T A FEELING, IT'S A CULTURE

Respect would seem to be among the most obvious of virtues. Nearly every single manager, if asked, would probably say that he or she respects his or her employees and customers. But the values between a respect-driven organization and a blame-driven organization ultimately come through in everyday decisions and interactions. These values start at the top and define who you are in the marketplace. A culture of respect is contagious, and how a workplace treats its employees ultimately mirrors how it treats its customers, its suppliers, and the surrounding community. This, in turn, often creates or destroys the mind-share that drives your market growth, as in the case of one firm that transcended a mature and crowded market with its own unique employee philosophy.

ROTH STAFFING: Redefining the Temp

The temporary help business is not normally a place where you would find the hottest growth company of 1999—particularly in southern California, home to hundreds of staffing agencies. But **Roth Staffing,** a placement firm headquartered in Brea, California, became another leader of the *Inc* 500 despite a business landscape that was at the height of the dot-com frenzy. In a crowded marketplace, its core competency has been an underlying respect for both its clients and its temporary employees.

In a business where most agencies send over applicants and collect fees, Roth gets to know its clients—in some cases, even establishing on-site offices to provide a complete, turnkey staffing solution. By understanding the operations of its customers, it becomes part of their team and not just a service provider. At the same time, Roth has high standards for these clients. It monitors their safety records and work environment, and in some cases have even dropped sites as customers rather than send its associates there. Perhaps most important, it has worked hard to dispel the notion of the temp. Premier associates are guaranteed at least 35 hours of work per week, plus benefits and a career path. Today, Roth's affiliates have more than 70 offices in several states, and the company grew over 20,000 percent over five years, with revenues in excess of $73 million per year.

People often view respect as an abstract value—a vaguely defined warm, fuzzy feeling towards people. But it is really a cultural value, and there is more science behind it than you might think. If you examine the daily operations of your workplace, respect gets measured in some very tangible ways:

- The authority people have to make decisions that cost money
- What happens when people make mistakes
- How many policies defend the employee's interest versus how many constrain it
- Whether people are measured for results versus following a process defined by others

In other words, respect is the by-product of how you handle many of the tough issues that crop up every day in the workplace—and the choices that create this respect aren't always the easy ones. It takes a conscious set of cultural values to create an atmosphere of respect, and buy-in at all levels of the organization to make it happen. Without these underlying values in place, a workplace sense of respect is too often conspicuous in its absence. The following example from my personal experience could easily be repeated in many of today's workplaces, in almost any industry.

OUR PEOPLE ARE IMPORTANT, BUT NOT IMPORTANT ENOUGH TO SERVE WELL

I had lunch once with a group of project managers for a major telecommunications firm. Their jobs, coordinating the installation of large voice and data networks for corporate clients, required them to travel frequently and spend long periods of time at customer sites. I asked them what they thought about their jobs, and the first thing they all brought up wasn't telecommunications, or travel, or customers—it was how the company required them to use their personal credit cards for all their travel expenses, and then took a very leisurely amount of time to reimburse them.

In the minds of these talented, hardworking people, the credit card situation seemed to be much more than a financial issue—it was a microcosm of an impersonal, Dilbert-like relationship between them and the organization. The fact that the company made it their problem to pay interest out of their own pockets on their personal credit cards equated to "it doesn't care"—and, in turn, they cared that much less about the interests of the company. And no one in any of this firm's corner offices would probably ever think to equate these feelings to things like morale, productivity, or turnover.

The road to a culture of disrespect is paved with decisions that seem good at the time, which in sum total gradually erode a previous level of trust. The restaurant that greets customers with a sign saying NO SUBSTITUTIONS, the hardware store with a sign saying ABSOLUTELY NO EMPLOYEES ALLOWED IN THIS OFFICE, or the corporate conglomerate that requires two signatures and a form in triplicate to order more notepads, all reacted to some real or imagined threat with a new rule. Then, given enough time, the rules take on a life of their own and become a culture.

This is not to imply that rules are a totally bad thing. Some are necessary safeguards against undesirable behavior, but others become part of the oral history of "who we are." So while sanctions against, for example, employee theft are generally understood and accepted, requiring an onerous amount of paperwork to approve something becomes cultural. Once you get past things you would expect to find in any human resources manual, and into the daily life of the workplace, the things you do and say become a reflection of your values towards employees and customers alike. Here are some of the core values that Motivators use to create a culture of respect:

Trust

A sense of trust is often at odds with business nature, because it is also at odds with human nature. We live in a world where absolute trust is unrealistic. Few if any businesses will leave cash unattended 24 hours per day, or tell people to help themselves to the products in the storeroom. Much of our lives revolve around setting boundaries with other people, from the locks on our doors to the terms of our contracts. But left unchecked, this natural sense of self-preservation can lead to a workplace that tacitly tells customers and employees, "We don't trust you, and we don't particularly like you, either."

Cultural values of trust imply a higher standard between an organization and its team members. Whether it is doing away with time clocks, providing flexible working arrangements, or giving your front line more responsibility, Motivators buy in to a formula that replaces your oversight with someone else's accountability. More important, these values replace rules with goals. Employees at retail legend Nordstrom, for example, are held to very high sales targets. To meet these goals, however, they have tremendous latitude in judgment to satisfy their customers. In general, cultures of trust focus more on results and less on making people march in lockstep to get there.

Individuality

Both people and organizations have a tendency to favor people like themselves—yet in reality, the most powerful teams are those whose talents complement each other. Motivators who respect individuality transcend the normal human urge towards self-perpetuation, and usually benefit in a big way from it.

Here as well, respect for individuality is much more than a feeling— there is a very tangible, structural aspect to it. To accommodate individuality, you often must design your workplace and its processes around the talents of a team, rather than around a homogenous group of like-minded people.

LESS-THAN-PERKY PEOPLE NEED NOT APPLY

It has become common practice within the call center industry to screen people for personality, under the assumption that hiring nothing but perky, congenial types of people will produce great service. My experience in managing a software customer support center has been exactly the opposite. Different personalities provide clear advantages in specific situations—a taciturn analytical thinker, for example, will make some customers much happier than Ms. Congeniality when a complex problem is at hand.

Harnessing the talents of a diverse team of people requires developing specialties and subspecialties that allow everyone to play to their strengths and be important. In this support center, people who taught well would serve as training coordinators, others who were very organized became liaisons to the company's product development team, while our top computer hotshots indulged themselves by having others escalate the toughest technical problems to them. And all of them were trained extensively on how to communicate well with customers, with exactly the same personalities that they had coming in. The results were near perfect customer satisfaction ratings and a support team that became the most highly rated aspect of the company.

Diversity

The classic concept of diversity revolves around external characteristics such as race, gender, religion, or sexual orientation. Sadly, there are still old boy networks that embrace diversity only to the extent forced on them by law. Such environments are gradually going the way of the dinosaur, for competitive as well as legal reasons. But there is a more subtle aspect as well. Respect implies a diversity of viewpoints, personalities, and interests. The organization where prospective salespeople need to know who quarterbacks the New York Giants, for example, is at a cultural disadvantage in the market against firms whose salespeople simply know how to sell well—unless your organization happens to be the New York Giants.

For Motivators, the cornerstone of a culture of diversity is the thirst to find talent in whatever packages they come in. These are cultures who reach out to underrepresented groups in search of talent. Wegmans, for instance, recruits inner-city youth from its home base of Rochester, New York, for a scholarship program tied in with employment at Wegmans, and the program generates high success rates with minimal turnover. Other cultures find innovative ways to accommodate physically challenged team members, or encourage women and minorities to pursue careers in their firms' professions. Welcoming any person with the right skills and cultural fit, and treating them equally inside the organization, is a necessary prerequisite for all other forms of workplace respect.

Dealing with Problems

Be honest with yourself. When something goes wrong in your workplace, what gets fixed first, the problem or the blame? Human nature is protective by definition, and its instinct is to blame people and cover up responsibility. Conversely, the level of respect in your culture gets defined at those moments when it is the most difficult to walk the talk, as the whole world once observed following the *Challenger* space shuttle tragedy.

THE CHALLENGER INCIDENT: Speak No Evil

After the space shuttle *Challenger* exploded on liftoff in 1986, killing seven astronauts, subsequent congressional hearings revealed that engineers at rocket manufacturer **Morton Thiokol** had strongly advised against a cold-weather launch, because launch temperatures were well below the known performance threshold of the rocket booster's O-ring seals. Yet the launch went forward with the approval of Thiokol's management, over the engineers' objections, because of a misguided belief that it would be OK to "push the envelope" of the design specifications.

During these hearings, two key Thiokol engineers were pressured by management to restrict their testimony to simple "yes" or "no" answers, and to reveal as little information as possible. Instead, they took their oath to tell "the whole truth" literally, and revealed the full scope of their prelaunch technical concerns. Both were demoted or reassigned by their company shortly afterwards—one later became reinstated as a company spokesperson following congressional pressure and bad publicity, while the other soon left the aerospace industry for good.

Your style in dealing with major problems is usually predetermined by how you handle daily business life. Human nature is to criticize mistakes as incompetence, but coaching people to improve within a blame-free environment takes more work. Human nature is to protect yourself from criticism, but respect demands openness with yourself and others. Above all, human nature sees people as the problem, while the values of a Motivator help you see these same people as part of the solution instead.

Putting Employees First

Most important, your level of respect reflects a fundamental stance that an organization has towards its employees. This stance shows itself in your response to both great and small events in your daily business life:

- When a company takes every step possible to preserve jobs in a downturn, instead of simply viewing employees as faceless liabilities to be jettisoned
- When an employee becomes disabled, and a business goes above and beyond basic legal requirements to accommodate the employee's return to work
- On more of an everyday basis, when you support your team's personal and family commitments instead of demanding ceaseless overtime

Every week, month, and year brings moments of truth where one choice would be most expedient for the business and the other would be in the best interests of the employees. It is within these moments that Motivators define a culture of respect in the eyes of their teams. This culture has a long-term payoff that can be tangibly seen in the market leadership of many employee-oriented companies. Conversely, there is a price to be paid for ignoring your employee interests. For example, during the collapse of energy giant Enron—once one of the country's highest-rated employers—the public outcry over executives cashing out their stock while employees were forced to helplessly watch their pension funds sink has become an enduring image of bad corporate behavior.

Respect in the workplace ultimately has a deeper dimension beyond daily business practices. It bespeaks how much people in a workplace love their jobs and care about the welfare of the organization. It is a goal that everyone aspires to, which has tangible benefits in areas such as productivity, turnover, and innovation. The fact that it requires a fresh set of workplace values to happen represents a strategic advantage for organizations with successful cultures, because the road to creating respect is harder and more subtle than most people realize.

AUTONOMY ON THE FRONT LINES:
Getting beyond Command-and-Control

Anyone who has left their teenagers home alone for the first time, or entrusted a mission-critical project to their employees, understands why frontline autonomy is not a natural instinct. It is a cultural groundwork that must be laid far in advance. But when Motivators respect the roles of their own employees, and give them the responsibility and authority to make the right decisions, it sends a powerful message about their importance to the team—as highlighted in one recent episode that took place at a snack-food manufacturer.

LETTING THE PRODUCTION TEAM MAKE THE CALL

An employee at a major snack-food plant once found part of a glass bottle that had made its way down the assembly line. This was a potentially serious situation, because of the risk that pieces of glass from the rest of the bottle could have made their way into bags of their product. An emergency meeting was convened of all their production employees, and at this meeting, the plant's management made two unforgettable gestures. First, they asked the production workers to recommend, as a team, how the plant should respond. Second, they agreed without hesitation to the team's recommendation—to destroy two full shifts' worth of production, involving more than $40,000 of food products, to prevent even the slightest chance of a problem.

Every manager's ideal is to have employees who act like owners and who put the company's interests ahead of their personal ones. A critical ingredient in achieving this is how much authority your frontline team has in performing its jobs. The degree to which your teams have the attitude of an owner correlates directly with your commitment to their having the autonomy of an owner.

Like most great cultural values, this runs counter to human nature. The first impulse of a manager is to manage: to tell other people what to do and how to do it. And ceding that authority to subordinates can feel like handing the asylum keys to the inmates. Putting results in the hands of your team feels a lot less safe than simply making it follow a predefined process. This fundamental conflict is part of the reason why many employees do not feel like owners, even when they *are* the owners.

EMPLOYEE-OWNED DOESN'T ALWAYS MEAN EMPLOYEE-FRIENDLY

When Gerald Greenwald was the CEO of **United Airlines,** he struggled to change many of the management practices at this "employee-owned" air carrier. For example, he instituted required training on employee relations for its middle management, to spread the word that "the days you could supervise with a two-by-four, shouting at employees and treating them like serfs were over." But as he puts it, there was often an attitude of, "You change first, and then I'll think about changing," dating back to a labor-management style that long predated his tenure.

When Greenwald made these observations in his recent book *Lessons from the Heart of American Business,* he concluded that it's hard to change an ingrained culture overnight, even when you usher in a new era of employee ownership. Today, United still languishes near the bottom of the industry in customer satisfaction ratings, and during the summer of 2000, slowdowns by its pilots and machinists created massive flight delays and cancellations—ironically sending United's stock price tumbling for these same employee-owners.

Perhaps the most telling point is how management culture transcends even the structure of a business. United is now owned by its employees—effectively, by its unions—but despite employee representation up to the board of directors level, it has not been a hotbed of employee satisfaction.

Southwest Airlines, by comparison, is a traditional unionized carrier owned by stockholders, just like many of its more poorly rated brethren. But key differences in the philosophy exist on the front lines, and Southwest's employees buy in to that philosophy. Southwest management often states that "the customer comes second," after its employees, yet its focus on employee autonomy and responsibility has resulted in some of the highest service quality ratings in the industry.

Like many cultural values, greater team autonomy starts with a set of underlying business decisions. Some of the factors that help Motivators foster a culture of autonomy include:

Team Involvement in Business Processes

In a recent television commercial, a CEO is at a company meeting, rallying people behind a new strategy that has the enthusiastic support of upper management. Then people from the information technology department, who had apparently never been consulted, speak up one by one, stating that this strategy will be impossible to implement. As the CEO's face falls, someone asks sarcastically if he's still so enthusiastic.

The popularity of frontline involvement in business decisions seems to rise and fall with cycles of popular business thought. It was once popular in management circles to foster a group decision-making process involving all levels of the team. Later, during the rash of 1990s downsizing, others theorized that only decision makers at the top were capable of making painful choices. Today, following the throes of a labor shortage, team involvement is again starting to make a comeback. While this pendulum continues to swing back and forth to the present day, one overall concept is clear: no one knows more about a business process than the people performing it. Their input and involvement are critical to both their morale and your success, and can only be ignored at your peril.

Team Responsibility for Results

One firm once gathered its employees together, took a stack of 100 one-dollar bills of "revenue," and then parceled out where each of those dollars went, so that people understood the need to make the best of a tight profit margin in their daily work. At a deeper level, Motivators go far beyond telling employees what to do and focus them on meeting goals. For example, FedEx assigns a team of people to unload each of its arriving aircraft in as little as 18 minutes, depending on the size of the aircraft, and if the team goes even one minute over, the causes are discussed in a daily troubleshooting meeting at the end of the shift. As a result, people on the ramp clearly understand their role in the end product of delivering a package "absolutely, positively overnight."

The key here is to tie authority to responsibility, with enough feedback to allow people to measure their own performance. Many automakers, for instance, now employ cross-functional teams of assembly workers, with overall responsibility for a specific part of the vehicle assembly process. Compared with the traditional assembly line, this process motivates people to be responsible for the quality of an overall functional area, and not just dispassionately tighten the same bolt all day. The closer that employees are to the ultimate goals of your business, and the more responsibility you give each of them for reaching these goals, the more that people will harness their natural instincts to pull together as a team.

Peer Oversight versus Manager Oversight

The concept of a peer team leader or coach, or even a self-managed team, is reinforced by important performance psychology. Logic would tell most managers to measure performance and then coach people who need improvement. While this approach may make sense theoretically, the real world is a little different. When bosses measure the performance of subordinates and coach them, the innate response is often to cover one's derriere. When peer groups take responsibility for basic performance instead, the focus shifts from avoiding blame to improving the process—and to maintaining the respect of their peer group.

Peer team leadership is an important component of team autonomy. At software vendor The CBORD Group, for example, individual team leaders—who are not supervisors—take responsibility for scheduling and work-flow management within their groups of five to ten people. Other peers are responsible for call quality monitoring and coaching, while still others coordinate internal training. The result is a tightly knit group that has experienced almost no turnover and that maintains excellent customer satisfaction ratings. On a larger scale, peer responsibility forms an important part of the leadership development process in any work environment and helps feed the pipeline for a strong promote-from-within environment.

Putting more autonomy in the hands of a team takes work, and trust. This is not the usual way that most workplaces operate, which means that implementing it often requires gradual change, time, and oversight. But when it works, the change can be dramatic. More important, greater levels of autonomy move an organization's managers into more strategic roles, working as a team with the front line rather than baby-sitting it. A culture of autonomy gives people the pride they deserve in working well, and lets them harness this energy to the entire team's benefit.

PERSONAL CAREER GROWTH AND MOBILITY

The number one reason that employees leave frontline positions isn't money or status. It is lack of training and advancement opportunities. In this sense, work is not just a destination, but a journey. People are naturally concerned about things like how much money is in their paycheck, but statistically, they are even more concerned with how important their contributions are, and where they will go in the future. Motivators who foster a sense of personal growth reap benefits both in practical areas such as turnover and in more subtle ones such as commitment and performance level.

Personal growth follows an individual path for each person on a team—one may wish to be recognized as a leader and advance, another may seek a degree or diploma in night school, while others may simply want to be secure and appreciated within their positions. For any person, you can break down desires like these into three ingredients for a culture of personal growth:

1. The ability to learn
2. The ability to grow
3. The ability to succeed

Each of these areas represents a win-win situation that succeeds only with conscious effort to make them part of your culture. Learning requires an investment of time if not resources, growth requires planning for career paths and use of skills, and success requires a reward structure for people who add value to your business. However, each of them represents opportunities for a strong culture to attract and keep its best people.

The Ability to Learn

In the animated movie *Toy Story,* as soon as a group of toys are left alone, the first thing they do is call a staff meeting and thank one of the participants for leading a seminar on plastics. The urge to continue learning is universal, no matter what business you are in. Continuing lifelong learning not only teaches important information, but also makes your team part of an ongoing higher purpose in the workplace. Motivators overinvest in learning to reap obvious benefits in skills and productivity, but also to create a culture that says, "You are important."

USAA: A Focus on Lifelong Learning

At USAA, an insurance and financial services company serving current and former military officers, education and training are a way of life. The firm invests nearly 3 percent of its gross revenues in training—twice the industry average. It also invests in the college educations of nearly a third of its employees, sponsoring up to one undergraduate and one graduate degree per employee, and, somewhat unusual, paying for this education up front, as well as providing on-site classroom space to local colleges to deliver it.

There is a direct relationship between USAA's training philosophy and its retention rates. Turnover is barely above 5 percent per year versus an industry average of 30 percent to 45 percent. More important, it drives a strong promote-from-within environment, where more than 40 percent of its employees are promoted each year, and leadership roles generally are filled from within the ranks.

This desire to learn has become even more of a critical competitive factor, now that a host of new interactive learning methodologies are taking shape. According to e-learning guru Elliott Masie, more than half of the companies he surveyed are now implementing an online learning strategy, and he feels that "a strong learning culture and delivery capability are an incredible competitive advantage in these tougher times. The amount of training and learning will increase in coming years." (Putting his money where his mouth is, Masie himself now delivers a substantial percentage of his keynote speaking engagements "virtually," via online technology, from his home base in Saratoga Springs, New York.)

While companies once copied training handouts and passed them around in classrooms, today even the humblest of firms can deploy learning content in real time to thousands of people using tools such as the Internet. And even within traditional classroom approaches, there is more to know than ever in today's business environment. These trends mean more choices for a strong learning strategy, and an even greater need to make it part of your culture.

The Ability to Grow

Motivators seek ways for the individual to add value and become important. This creates a strong buy-in, where cultural values become team-driven rather than management-driven.

Providing growth opportunities for your team sometimes requires taking a fresh look at the whole value equation within your workplace. Many organizations see the world in terms of a linear organization chart, with junior and senior levels of responsibility. At the same time, the needs of your business and the talents of your people may call for a broader level of career opportunities. By looking closely at who brings what value into the workplace, strong cultures often find that cultivating expertise in nontraditional career paths helps build a much stronger team, as with the case of some firms who have created senior roles for their key technical talent.

PUTTING TECHNICAL PEOPLE AT THE TOP

Because a common complaint of top technical people is that their careers eventually stall unless they move into management, some forward-looking firms have developed a culture where technical and management career paths run parallel, rather than simply having one sit on top of another. For example, numerous firms such as **Boeing, FedEx, Northrop Grumman,** and others have created senior level "technical fellow" positions. These positions generally have greater research and development autonomy, a mentoring role within the company, and a rank commensurate with upper management. As a result, these firms have successfully retained many of their best minds, some of whom have fueled a continuing stream of innovations that have helped them remain on top of their industries.

The key to providing growth opportunities is helping people to align their goals with an increased value to your organization. Could you afford to promote every single person on your current team right now? If the result was increased output, productivity, expertise, and service quality, perhaps you could. In addition, the costs of turnover mean that keeping one relatively well-compensated person is often more cost-effective than continually rehiring several people who receive smaller paychecks. One trait that many of the best cultures share in common is higher-than-average paychecks *and* profits. By looking carefully at how people add value at work, you can often create a similar win-win situation in your own culture.

The Ability to Succeed

Man is a goal-seeking creature, and Motivators provide a reward structure that facilitates people reaching their personal and professional goals within the workplace. And as often as not, these goals are not financial. Work represents more than half of most people's waking lives, and many of us seek meaning and fulfillment within our life's work. Whether it is a good paycheck, or recognition of peers, good cultures must provide people the opportunity to succeed on their own terms.

ARE YOU A CREATIVE PARADOX?

How many people have a job title of "Creative Paradox"? Or "Chief Morale Officer"? Or "Technical Bigshot"? These are just a few examples of cultures who have fit a specific role to an individual, rather than vice versa. The first example was the title that **Hallmark Cards** gave the late author Gordon MacKenzie towards the end of his 30-year career there, as he rose from the ranks of their greeting-card artists to become a mentor helping others find their places within the firm's culture. These and other titles represent roles that gave specific people opportunity to use talents, and deliver benefits, that you rarely find on a typical organization chart.

When people do their best on behalf of your organization, they are essentially giving you a gift. Acknowledging and nurturing these gifts is essential to receiving more of them in the future. When employees say, "Nobody notices me unless I foul something up," it is a danger signal that life revolves around duty and not success. And the same is true if your employee performance reviews focus on laundry lists of good deeds and bad deeds, instead of on a vision for the future—or worse, if these reviews appear late or not at all. Conversely, Motivators foster a culture of personal and professional success that recognizes each person's contribution to the team and the organization.

Personal career growth is one of the most tangible expressions of a culture that values its people. In turn, this growth can spawn a level of commitment and dedication that you could never easily hire off the street. Above all, making it happen requires more than simply carving out slots on an organization chart. It starts with getting to know the people on your team as individuals with unique strengths and talents, and then looking strategically at how to harness these talents for the good of the organization. Handled well, it can go far beyond external factors like turnover and productivity, into the dedication and commitment people have to your culture's success.

TAKING A FRESH LOOK AT MOTIVATION

Every business would like to motivate its employees. The term itself, however, can be misleading. Its linguistic roots *(to move)* imply bringing some external force to bear that will change people. But in reality, motivation occurs naturally as the result of groundwork that is laid far in advance—it is a by-product of a good workplace and rarely just a reaction to an event. This means that the path to motivation starts long before one might think about bringing in a speaker, a training program, or a corporate initiative, and it begins right in your own backyard.

Ultimately, the cultural values behind a positive workplace—respect, autonomy, and personal growth—represent the essence of true motivation. And the good news is that none of them are just fuzzy, vaguely defined concepts that are hard to implement. They simply require a different mind-set going forward, as you make the same daily business decisions that everyone else must make. Best of all, creating this positive workplace usually requires more of an investment of spirit than of money.

When you become a Motivator and make the commitment to a new relationship between yourself and your team, you join an exclusive fraternity. Often it is one that trades the easy or expedient choices for the sake of strong working relationships, and, in return, trades short-term costs for long-term profits. It is a win-win situation for both parties that simply starts with a new perspective towards the workplace. And once you succeed in building this new relationship, you will find that you have tapped into a boundless source of energy that is hidden from most businesses—the enthusiasm and innovation of your own people.

Wendy's

People Are Their Recipe

When you have a restaurant concept that scales to more than 6,000 locations worldwide, how do you foster a culture of respect for your employees? For Wendy's, the third-largest quick-service restaurant chain in the world, the answer revolves around how you cook a hamburger. Its operations are a microcosm of how a system can be designed to be customer-centric, and built around teamwork.

When Kentucky Fried Chicken franchisee Dave Thomas decided to enter the crowded hamburger business in the late 1960s, fast-food restaurants were traditionally built on a model of stockpiling an inventory of sandwiches and then selling them. By comparison, the fledgling restaurant chain Thomas named after his daughter's nickname, "Wendy," was built from day one around preparing food to order, on demand. It is an efficient way to work, but more important, it fosters a sense of team results and individual importance, because the successful execution of a customer order depends on the involvement of almost every person behind the counter. Today, with nearly $8 billion in annual revenues and the highest growth rate of any major fast-food chain, Wendy's philosophy still drives the operations of the entire company as well as the restaurants themselves.

What sets Wendy's apart from other quick-service restaurants is its focus on people: in a business that is well known for high turnover, it has better overall morale, retention, and service quality than many of its competitors. In part, this springs from the attitude at the top of the company—its late founder Thomas was often fond of telling people, "I'm just a hamburger cook," and his values drove an upper management that champions the interests of the people on the front lines. More important, its cultural value of teamwork has spread over time to areas such as above-average levels of training, employee development, and benefits—ranging from paid vacations to a stock option plan for managers and supervisors, both unusual in the fast-food industry.

According to Jeff Coghlan, who is a partner in one of Wendy's largest franchise groups, "The whole idea behind our concept is built-to-order, one customer at a time, and the difference is amazing. For one thing, everyone at every level of our operations knows how to do things—our president could walk in and work the grill. At other chains, I'd see multiunit managers put on a suit and that was the end of their food-handling days. Another thing is the teamwork here—it's critical in our operation. Part of the reason we have a more palpable culture than many of our competitors is that we are very much an assembly line, and if we don't work together the whole line shuts down." As he sees it, frontline virtues such as cross-functional training, coaching, and covering for your teammates aren't just nice concepts, they are the lifeblood of its operations. Wendy's business model requires everyone to succeed, and therefore enforces that ethic as a culture.

The side effects of having a team environment with high standards find their way into many other aspects of the firm's operations, which, in turn, helps Wendy's restaurants define who they are:

- *Execution.* As Coghlan points out, "In the Wendy's business, you have to be much more aware of exactly what is going on at the moment. There are time goals for literally everything we do, whether it's cleaning a window, or doing a trash run, or cutting onions. And in sandwich preparation, it's single-digit seconds. The same goes for precision: if the fries and the drink and the sandwich all don't hit the tray at the same time, then the two people who got it right haven't accomplished anything. But we take pride in our execution, and even the newest employees understand their own importance to this and buy in." Today, surveys show that the company still maintains the fastest speed of service ratings in the quick-service restaurant industry by a large margin.
- *Training.* Wendy's corporate headquarters provides an extensive training curriculum, with courses ranging from recruiting and time management all the way to a formal management development program. In addition, it maintains ongoing certification programs in areas such as cleanliness, speed, and operating standards, where the whole restaurant team becomes part of the process of meeting and maintaining these standards. Its Service Excellence program, for example, now in

its fourth year, measures very specific standards designed around a positive guest experience.

- *Continuous improvement.* Over time, Wendy's has successfully automated many of the scut work tasks of a fast-food operation, with nearly a full workday of dishwashing and bun preparation saved per day in recent years by new processes. During the years, this focus on operating standards has led to innovations in other areas: Wendy's was the first, for example, to introduce the scoreboards that verify drive-through orders as the customers watch. There is a strong leadership component even in entry-level positions, with individual employees taking personal responsibility for specific operations.

- *Concern for employees.* Wendy's has a vested interest in everyone being able to perform well, and some of Wendy's franchisees also offer benefits such as an employee-assistance program, helping any restaurant employee with concerns ranging from substance abuse to elder care and legal issues. In general, Wendy's and its franchisees see benefits as both a recruiting and a retention tool. According to one of its human resources managers, "Many fast-food restaurants keep people under a certain number of hours so they don't have to pay benefits. We go out of our way to make sure the managers in the restaurants have health insurance and other benefits, and that makes a big difference in whether your key people stay with you."

In a very real sense, Wendy's culture also reflects the personality of its late founder, Dave Thomas. During his lifetime, he became an American cultural icon for his homespun television commercials (he made more than 700, making him the most prolific figure in advertising history), as well as his bestselling book *Dave's Way.* Privately, he was a hard-driven businessman with high standards, particularly when it came to Wendy's "guests." Above all, his personal values were those of his company, and two of his favorite messages to colleagues were "Just treat people nice" and "Do the right thing." On his passing in 2002, many Wendy's corporate employees described him as the greatest influence in their lives—and the current management team is strongly committed to Thomas's ideals moving forward to the future. At a tangible level, this drives an organization that continues to have unusually strong relationships with employees, franchisees, and customers alike.

The Wendy's corporate slogan of "Quality is our recipe" applies as much to its people as to its hamburgers. Franchisee Coghlan puts it well: "We're in an industry that gets maligned constantly. But our managers go in and make people proud of what we're doing—and appreciate the level of difficulty, the level of teamwork, the level of sophistication that is required of them. Sometimes when I hear someone say, 'Well, I could always flip hamburgers,' I scratch my head and say to myself, 'I doubt it.' But the people we have are excited about what they do, they are proud of what they do, and they get their satisfaction from their guests who express it." As a result, Wendy's continues to be one of the success stories of the food-service industry—in its fourth decade and counting.

4

The Team Builders
Getting the Best from Your Human Capital

Team Builders feel that the most important investment they can make is in their people. As a result, they put more emphasis on recruiting and human development strategies than most of their competitors do. Team Builders see their organizations as people who serve each other as "internal customers," who in turn provide the same excellent service to their external customers. Some of the principles that set them apart include the following:

Our projects often cross departmental boundaries. Major automakers such as Ford and DaimlerChrysler, for example, often base new vehicle projects around interdisciplinary teams, with participants ranging from designers to finance people. These professionals work for the vehicle team, and not for their home departments, for the duration of the project. This approach has helped shorten the lead time for designing a new automobile, and has served as a model worldwide for the dynamics of team working environments.

We have a very structured recruiting process with substantial team involvement. Perhaps the hardest job at the Ritz-Carlton hotel chain is getting hired. Potential employees are screened using a "character trait recruiting" system involving a detailed personality profile, as well as several rounds of interviews. This system not only drives the chain's industry-leading levels of customer satisfaction, but has reduced turnover by 50 percent in what is now a very strong team working environment.

People are primarily evaluated on how well they serve others in the organization. Once upon a time, only one person evaluated your performance—your immediate supervisor. Today, organizations are increasingly adopting so-called "360-degree" performance reviews, where your value to each person you serve internally is assessed. Tools like these help reinforce the concept of "internal customer relationships" and how important they are to the success of the enterprise.

If you had a choice between individuals narrowly doing their jobs or a team focused on meeting your goals, which would you choose? The team model is an attractive concept, which often breaks down in the harsh light of individual demands and responsibilities. It is also a concept that has evolved over time from its simplistic beginnings of joint responsibility and rewards to become the cornerstone of many firms' operations. An essential component of Team Building cultures is the ability to band together for the sake of common organizational goals and to execute as a team.

Many subtle, underlying cultural values lie behind the success or failure of work teams. They start with how a team is formed initially, including the methodology used to hire and recruit people, and an assessment of culture fit. From there, they involve fundamental issues in areas such as how people are rewarded, how much responsibility and autonomy they are given, and how they deal with the organization as a whole—and delve deeper into the intrinsic motivations that drive each person's work life.

Many workplaces move into using teams with great fanfare, and then unknowingly sabotage them by withholding authority or management support, or by trying to force-fit a team model on a traditional departmental culture. Conversely, Team Builders leave job and department boundaries and "turf" behind to focus on what is of most value to the organization.

When the team model works well, its impact on productivity, morale, and culture in general can be profound. Here we will examine how teams are built, why they succeed and fail, and how team environments are implemented in successful cultures.

BUILDING THE RIGHT TEAM: Hiring and Recruiting

Hiring drives your corporate culture. Who joins your team and how you recruit them has perhaps the biggest influence on who your organization is and how well you ultimately succeed. The values that drive successful hiring are often contrarian, such as hiring for aptitude versus skills, making a higher investment in initial training, and placing as much hiring authority in the workgroup as possible. Values like these are what ultimately set Team Building cultures far apart from the average workplace, and hiring and recruiting practices are among the more visible differences between these organizations and typical ones—as evidenced by one of the more successful grocery chains in the United States.

WEGMANS: a Focus on Recruiting and Retention

Wegmans, with stores throughout the northeastern United States, has become one of the success stories of the retail grocery industry. It is consistently rated as having one of the highest service quality ratings of any supermarket chain, and is one of the top retailers listed among the 100 Best Companies to Work For in America by *Fortune* magazine. Keeping a steady stream of talented employees is important to any retailer the size of Wegmans, with more than 30,000 employees serving over 60 stores, but an even greater challenge is consistently attracting the kind of people that will maintain its best-of-class service quality and work environment.

Wegmans takes a unique approach to attracting and retaining its people. First of all, in an industry that employs many part-time personnel, Wegmans is one of few chains to offer benefits such as health insurance, paid vacations, and dependent-care reimbursement accounts to all its employees. In addition to benefits, it offers a third-party resource and referral service called Workplace Connections to assist employees with personal needs such as arranging child care. And to meet ongoing hiring and training needs, the chain has taken the unusual step of having a full-time human resources professional in each store.

Perhaps the crown jewel of Wegmans's approach to hiring and retaining good people is its scholarship program. Any Wegmans employee who meets minimum academic requirements and job performance standards, and presents a clear case for his or her goals and objectives, can apply for a scholarship that pays half of the college tuition up to a maximum of $1,500 per year. During the past 17 years, more than 13,000 employees have received scholarships totaling approximately $44 million, and many have moved into full-time professional positions with the company following graduation.

Team Building cultures are hard to get into—top firms may receive more than 200 résumés for every open position, and companies such as Internet hardware vendor Cisco now receive more than 100,000 résumés each month. For the fortunate ones who are considered for positions, there is generally a more structured approach to the process of candidate selection. Thus, one of the side effects of building a great workplace culture is a strong candidate pool, in nearly any job market condition, and also your culture literally begins with the best practices in the recruitment process. Here are some guidelines for putting these best practices in place within your own Team Building efforts.

Value Aptitude over Pedigree

Many years ago, I personally faced a choice between hiring two candidates for a software development position. One had completed a Ph.D. from a respected university, and her thesis was on exactly the topic we were hiring for. The other was a former coal miner who had recently retrained himself in computer programming. Which one would you choose?

I followed my instincts instead of the résumés and hired the coal miner. As luck would have it, our company offered another position to the other candidate as well, and the results confirmed my gut suspicions. The person with the Ph.D. was an average performer who contributed few new ideas, while the former coal miner turned out to be one of the most intelligent and creative employees we have ever hired. His raw aptitude for learning new things, troubleshooting problems, and taking project responsibility eventually made him the chief technical architect of our company's next generation product.

Today, more organizations are starting to *seek raw talent first and then invest in a higher level of training to develop that talent.* This trend is particularly evident in the technology industry, where labor shortages and rapid change have all but demanded a fresh look at nontraditional job candidates. This trend, however, has frequently been an ingrained value all along in companies with Team Building cultures. They realize that their best people are not necessarily the ones with the longest alphabet soup of credentials, but the ones with the greatest aptitudes to learn and grow.

APTITUDE—THE KEY TO TECHNICAL HIRING

According to an Information Technology Association of America study, more than 800,000 positions in the information technology (IT) field were unfilled in the year 2001, and even with a slowing economy, only half of these positions were expected to be filled within the next year. This hot IT job market has led to sometimes frantic bidding for talent, including one company who even leased new BMWs as perks for incoming employees. It has also spawned an environment where it is not unusual for IT professionals to hop to new jobs every 12 to 18 months for more money or benefits.

But one firm, software security vendor **Cigital, Inc.,** has built and retained a staff of more than 40 technical people without even so much as running ads or paying recruiter fees. Its secret: hiring people based on referrals from current employees and college faculty contacts, and then screening them for basic problem-solving ability versus current software skills. Once hired, new technical employees go through extensive training in the company's software and security technologies. CEO Jeffrey Payne, whose company now has become one of the 500 fastest-growing companies in America, views this training as a long-term investment in the company's success. The proof of the pudding: almost no turnover within its technical staff.

In Team Building cultures, a candidate's past history on a résumé is less a measure of "what you did" than of "who you are," with specific experiences seen in the larger context of traits such as success, leadership, and responsibility. Experience is then measured against more intangible qualities, such as interest and attitude, that rarely come across on paper. This helps great cultures breed great people, instead of just people who can start working the soonest. In an aptitude-based recruiting environment, there is a keen sense that skills can be trained, while personalities and potential cannot.

Know Who You Are Hiring

In cases like the one mentioned previously, hiring for aptitude means accurately assessing which coal miner will succeed in your organization and which Ph.D. won't—and vice versa. Team Builders leverage a variety of assessment techniques to drive the process of bringing strong nontraditional candidates onto their teams, measuring everything from quantitative reasoning to cultural fit. Some, like the following resort developer, start from a perspective of how excited you are about what the company does.

ARE YOU INTO WHAT WE ARE INTO?

If you interview with Vancouver-based IntraWest Resorts, be prepared to spend a lot of time talking about hitting the slopes—or the golf links.

There is more than fun involved, however. IntraWest is a resort developer and operator that creates all-encompassing "villages" in ski, golf, and beach locations throughout North America that are designed to provide a seamless guest experience. Its dedicated recruiting Web site, <www.wework2play.com>, features an extensive discussion of the IntraWest culture, testimonials from existing employees, and a detailed explanation of specific jobs. Above all, it is designed to help candidates self-select for the traits they value the most—energy, enthusiasm, and a love of the sports that drive a nearly billion-dollar resort empire. In a recent interview, IntraWest's recruiting director underscored that it will often sacrifice experience for cultural fit, but that to succeed there, you really need to be into its sports.

Now tools and methodologies allow for better candidate selection than ever before. Key players include psychological testing firms, business consultants, and even temporary help firms, some of whom are taking a growing role in the general employee assessment process. Many companies also use their own specific processes, ranging from work-sample testing to cultural "moments of truth." For example, a group of pilots interviewing at Southwest Airlines were once asked to shed their suits and wear company-issued Bermuda shorts (the one pilot who refused was not hired). At the higher end of the spectrum, other firms are turning to the Internet to further automate the front end of the candidate assessment process.

GETTING THE RECRUITING PROCESS ONLINE

If Development Dimensions International has its way in the marketplace, much of the employee screening process of the future will take place directly between the applicant and his or her computer screen. Their WebScreen tool assesses candidates using online profiling tests created from job information provided by the recruiter, measuring both specific skills and cultural fit. The results then can be used to steer promising candidates to further aptitude and motivational screening, direct applicants to other jobs they qualify for, or even give applicants the proverbial "don't call us, we'll call you" line online—all without human intervention.

On the recruiter side, WebScreen can create candidate-specific interview guides from the applicant's screening responses—the live interview that Joe eventually gets for the job may well differ from the one Sally gets, based on their performance online. DDI envisions the WebScreen tool as part of a broad-based virtual hiring process, ranging from video day-in-the-life previews of specific jobs to profiles that help candidates self-select appropriate career areas, all the way to the care and feeding of an ongoing database of job seekers. While some parts of the recruiting process may never be automated—including that one-on-one "gut feeling" that may ultimately seal a hiring decision—tools such as these may play a greater role in helping hiring managers get to that crucial one-on-one point more efficiently and accurately.

An even more important factor in maintaining a Team Building culture is to assess attitude as well as aptitude. Restaurateur Mark Campagnolo, who heads The Boatyard Grill restaurant profiled earlier, says that for his own recruiting, "Ninety percent of what we look for is attitude, and 10 percent is skills. We assess this attitude through how people communicate, and especially by what kinds of stories they relate. In particular, we always ask people to tell us about the funniest thing that's happened to them. A sense of humor is critical in this business; and we listen to see if they find the humor in their work experiences." On a broader scale, many firms now use some kind of attitudinal assessment, even turning to formal testing in some cases. On the other hand, many firms still just look at qualifications on a résumé, and give short shrift to the question of attitudinal fit—and often unwittingly lay the groundwork for a toxic workplace in the process.

Good cultures often employ a formal candidate assessment process today, and many bad ones do as well. One important difference lies in what is being screened for, and how valid the results are to the job: the quality of the hiring process often reflects the quality of all the other business processes within an organization. Most important, the best organizations realize that screening for cultural fit is as important as screening for eventual job performance.

Make Hiring a Team Process

What happens when you have more carefully screened, highly talented people in your organization? They act more like owners than employees, and they can play a more strategic role in an organization. Used properly, they can also help drive the hiring process, and perpetuate a team's culture and values. When you move to a team-based hiring approach, the focus often shifts from stock interview questions to a more accurate assessment of cultural fit within the work group.

SHOW US HOW YOU THINK

How many barbers are there in Chicago? How long would it take to move Mount Fuji? If we gave you a three-gallon pail and a five-gallon pail, how would you measure exactly four gallons of water into the larger one? If you are involved in a group interview nowadays, don't be surprised if you are asked "case" questions like these, designed to let the team observe how well you think on your feet in solving a nontrivial problem.

This trend is reputed to have begun with **Microsoft,** whose interviewees were once reportedly asked, "How many gas stations are there in America?" What interview teams often are looking for is the quality of the questions you ask in return, and how you interact with the group as you solve the problem. For instance, in the first example, you might explore how many men live in Chicago, how often they get their hair cut, how many hours per week the average barber spends cutting hair, allowances for vacations and sick time, and so forth. By the time you have solved the problem, the group has a better understanding of what it will be like to work with you in real life. (Incidentally, there are 4,140 barbers in Chicago as of this writing.)

Shifting from a management-driven hiring process to a team-based hiring process has become a major trend in industry today, and its benefits go far beyond the interview. Team members who feel that they have control over who can join their work group have a much stronger level of "ownership" in the culture of the team itself, as well as a greater stake in its ultimate success. Putting more hiring authority in the hands of your teams is often one of the best investments that an organization can make in the future of its workforce.

Retain Instead of Recruit

Team Building cultures know that the best way to recruit people is to do as little recruiting as possible—and keep more of the talent they already have. Turnover has real costs that can be as high as 150 percent of a departing person's annual salary, not to mention the effects on workload, morale, and further turnover. However, sometimes the worst thing an organization can do is start a formal "retention program."

HOW DO YOU REDUCE TURNOVER? ASK YOUR EMPLOYEES

A recent case study involving Time Warner Cable's Memphis, Tennessee, call center showed that a retention initiative involving higher pay, more levels of responsibility, and employee recognition had almost no impact on turnover. Finally, it let its own teams drive the process, and found out why people were really leaving—a five-year wait for promotions to day shift, coupled with a lack of evening child care, as well as management communications problems. By adjusting coverage hours and frankly addressing their team's involvement within the organization, turnover was ultimately reduced by nearly a third.

Beyond competitive compensation, Team Builders often look to other forms of "equity" for their employees, including career development and training, recognition and advancement, and flexible working arrangements. Food-service software vendor The CBORD Group, for instance, invests nearly three weeks of internal training per year for its call center employees, as well as initiatives like telecommuting arrangements that let many people "take their jobs with them" when a spouse relocates. This training begins the moment someone starts work—the company provides nearly ten weeks of initial training and call shadowing before someone actually takes a live phone call. The result? Turnover is so low that its software call center recently celebrated a year with no turnover among its 20-plus team—and even rehired the last person to leave shortly afterwards!

Retention has an impact far beyond the bottom line. When people are loyal to a company, and feel loyalty from it in return, there is an important ripple effect in fundamental business areas like experience, service quality, and ability to execute. More important, long employee tenures increase your competitiveness as an employer—when people see challenging long-term opportunities in a good working environment, it gives you a much richer pool of candidates to choose from when openings do occur. In a very real sense, Team Builders build their recruiting processes around what happens after someone is hired rather than before.

An organization's hiring practices involve much more than simply finding people to fill jobs. In a very real sense, they serve—or fail—as the corporate culture preservation department. This means that human resources is a very strategic function within the best companies, one that reaches far beyond being "the personnel department." The strategies behind building a company's human capital—and particularly the philosophies behind it—become an important part of what defines a Team Building organization.

The entire profession of human resources is undergoing a period of radical change. What was once, not many years ago, a process of reading mailed résumés and conducting verbal interviews has become a high-tech science encompassing databases, screening methodologies, and interacting with a worldwide audience on the Internet. At the same time, the human needs of adding quality employees hasn't changed—indeed, today's leaner competitive environments have made them even more critical. These two factors underscore the importance of putting recruiting in its proper place in an organization, as a key component of its underlying culture.

TEAM CULTURES VERSUS WORK GROUP CULTURES

Many firms make the mistake of assembling a group of people, calling them a "team," and ignoring the underlying values that will make them truly function as a team—authority, responsibility, and support from all levels of the management chain. Without these values, such partnerships are work groups who follow instructions, not teams in the true sense of the word. Just like their brethren in the sports world, workplace teams combine skills and good coaching with the responsibility to execute according to conditions on the field, and like sports champions, Team Building cultures function well by definition in a team environment. Here are some of the factors that differentiate a team from a work group:

Authority and Autonomy

Perhaps the central value of a team versus a work group is how much decision-making authority it has, and what autonomy it is granted to make these decisions. This is an important distinction, precisely because it tugs against the human nature within management that often leads to traditional command-and-control environments. People function better as a unified whole when they have more ownership of the process they perform, in almost any work environment—even the most repetitive manufacturing workplace.

MORE AUTONOMY AND TEAMWORK ON THE ASSEMBLY LINE

In many automotive assembly plants, work units are organized into functional teams, where each person on the team has the authority to stop an assembly line in the event of a quality problem. This approach grew in part from a need to make the assembly process more meaningful for its employees, which, in turn, drives competitive needs to build vehicles with higher quality and fewer defects.

Some automakers have taken the process a step further. One European automaker, for example, once experimented with making a team responsible for the assembly of an entire vehicle from start to finish. While the inherent inefficiency of using one team per vehicle eventually outweighed the advantages of this level of ownership, the lessons the industry learned from experiments like these have led to more of a team assembly process, with less of the Charlie Chaplin stereotype of people ceaselessly tightening the same bolt over and over.

There are naturally bounds to this autonomy, and workplace teams generally work under the same financial and productivity constraints as any group of employees. But a key difference is that they are treated as managers unto themselves, with the authority to make the best decisions within these constraints.

Responsibility for Results

This is an equally key litmus test for functioning as a team. If your responsibilities are to a process, you are a work group. If your responsibilities are to a set of results, you are a team. No matter how dedicated the individual contributors are, no group that has its every move precisely spelled out can truly call itself a team. Groups who are teams in the true sense of the word are given goals and objectives, not rules and procedures. Take, for example, when one major airline decided to share the rewards of running an on-time operation.

CONTINENTAL AIRLINES—IF WE'RE ON TIME, YOU GET A BONUS

Continental Airlines has a unique incentive for its employees: $65 per month in every employee's paycheck for each month that the airline meets its standards for on-time arrivals. (And the amount rises to $100 if it ranks first in on-time arrivals.) It is a simple technique that works, because people suddenly begin to care about the impact of their work on the overall goals of the airline. When ramp employees are late getting the baggage out, or the provisioning crew has problems delivering in-flight meals, it now attracts peer pressure as well as management concern. As a result, people execute better as a team, and Continental has delivered this bonus nearly every single month.

Elsewhere in the book, we discuss how some rewards can undermine motivation by replacing individual pride in performance with a financial carrot. By comparison, Continental's incentive works because it is based on the company's goals, rather than on individual performance. People are not given a bonus to do their jobs, but they share in the benefits when the company succeeds, which, in a higher sense, treats people like owners. In a similar sense, every workplace must find ways to help its employees take responsibility for results, and own the interests of the organization. (In Continental's case, the $3 million that it spends each month on bonuses, totaling nearly $100 million since 1995, represents less than half of the costs it used to incur by running late.)

Management Support

Perhaps the most important factor in a team's success is buy-in from affected management. It is one thing to say that you are in favor of teams and yet another to cede authority to people. Moreover, most managers today remain in charge of functional areas, and human nature makes it far too tempting for managers to pressure people to reach functional goals rather than team ones. Transcending these instincts requires a finely tuned intuition for long-term versus short-term success, as the automotive industry has learned over time.

LESSONS FROM WORKING AS A TEAM

Perhaps no industry has done more to promote teams than the automotive business has. As of this writing, some major automakers are entering their second decade and beyond of creating cross-disciplinary vehicle project teams versus the traditional approach of having functional groups, such as those handling body design, chassis, and electronics, each take turns designing their piece of the vehicle.

Over time, a lot of lessons have been learned from the team experiment. One is that it requires a fresh look at career paths. Some early team members found that they missed opportunities open to people who stayed put in vertical "chimney" organizations, and there is now more long-term planning for what happens with talented people during and after a team experience. Another is that it takes a concerted effort to avoid having team members pulled in different directions by their functional manager and their team. Perhaps most important was the discovery that certain personalities work better in teams than others do. Nowadays it is not unusual for potential team members to be screened by testing, simulation exercises, and interviews by psychologists. But the end result of all these efforts has been the most innovative and efficient era of automotive design in modern history.

Ultimately, the benefits of a team working environment requires a management that understands and buys in to the factors needed to make it work. They must understand that they will have to move beyond the natural instinct to protect their functional turf. Good management support for teams starts with an understanding of how they will benefit the management's own self-interest. Look critically at how teams will help you reach company-wide goals, examine what cultural changes will be needed to achieve these benefits, and then get everyone on board with the process.

Beyond these factors is a more intangible one, namely the individual motivations of the people on the team. Team Building environments work best when people's needs are filled by the emotional rewards of team goals. In the automotive industry examples previously mentioned, it was not unusual to find people working nights and weekends for the sake of their project teams, versus nine to five within their functional areas. The reason is simple: they were part of a small group accomplishing something very important, namely the design of an entire vehicle. To the extent that you can build importance into people's lives, the better your teams will function—and the stronger your culture will be. Ultimately, this sense of importance is perhaps the key value that drives the success of your teams.

THE GROWTH OF VIRTUAL TEAMS

No one would ever stop to think about the impact of the telephone on his or her culture of teamwork. Using telephones is as natural as breathing to most people, because telephones have been around for the entire lifetime of today's workforce. Yet their introduction created a radical change in the way that people could do business, compared to the days when people in remote locations were limited to sending text messages and paperwork between each other. In a very real sense, the telephone helped drive the growth of large, nationwide organizations by providing them a way to communicate immediately.

In much the same way, a new revolution is sweeping over today's Team Building environments—and once again, it is fueled by high-speed telecommunications. Computers and Internet tools now allow teams to share not only their voices, but data, images, sounds, and even their physical presence via video. A team of people scattered all over the world can gather around an electronic "chalkboard" and share ideas, draw on the same screen, or push Web pages or documents to each other—while all parties communicate verbally. Suddenly, it is as though people all over the world have had their desks moved into the same office.

Capabilities like these have been available to large companies for many years, and even today they are still most commonly found among firms that make substantial use of technology. But make no mistake, they will become as common as the telephone in time. These capabilities not only represent more convenience, but are an agent for cultural change in the workplace, as with my experience with distributed employees.

REMOTE TEAM MEMBERS—A PERSONAL PERSPECTIVE

I have been personally involved in efforts to network remote employees at the call centers of two software firms. By using telecommunications and customer relationship management software, an employee in Kansas City, for example, can seamlessly receive inbound calls from a call center in Los Angeles, with customer data popping up on the remote agent's computer just as though the agent were at headquarters. More important, agents do not work in isolation. From the comfort of their home offices, they can conference with other agents around the country, escalate calls to supervisors, or tap into online knowledge bases to solve customer issues.

These capabilities have greatly changed the nature of a work group at these call centers. Aside from allowing team members to work in multiple cities, these technologies have also created a true nationwide "virtual community." Team meetings take place via speakerphone, group training sessions take place over the Internet, and at regular get-togethers where remote agents travel to headquarters, people socialize like they have been working together all year, because, in a very real sense, they have. One product group now has a remote employee as a team leader, overseeing the work of a team based at headquarters. And even though some remote agents admit to occasionally working in their pajamas from their home offices, operations and service quality have tangibly improved for both call centers since they went virtual.

The deeper cultural issue behind virtual teams, in any industry, is freeing people from the normal bounds of time and distance. For many business environments, the watercooler conversation has been supplanted for good by teleconferences from Atlanta and e-mails from Amsterdam. More important, this newfound virtuality frees businesses from the bounds of regional or national culture. Nowadays it is not at all unusual for business initiatives to be in the hands of a global team of people, linked electronically, and sharing ideas and viewpoints from their respective home bases. As a result, companies can listen to the voices of more markets and business styles than ever before, and blend them in with their own culture.

These technologies are quickly becoming an integral part of our business lives, because they inherently save money and resources as they draw people closer together. And as with any cost-saving advances, they can become either swords or plowshares, to be used or misused depending on the underlying values of the firms who employ them. One firm may use them to create global project teams, while another may use them to move their already-underpaid service centers offshore to third-world countries to save costs, and yet another may exploit them to tap new markets and customers. Above all, the move towards virtual workplaces is here to stay. These trends are giving businesses tremendous power in how they manage their professional and human relationships, and this power is changing the fabric of teamwork for good.

THE CONCEPT OF THE INTERNAL CUSTOMER

People often view their jobs as simply performing job functions, such as assembling a component or serving a customer. But in reality, each and every one of us also serves other people inside an organization. For example, the assembler is serving the groups who use his or her components, the people who serve customers also serve the groups who profit from these customer transactions, and in a very real sense, upper management serves everyone else in an organization. These *internal* customer relationships are often just as critical to your success as are external ones.

One of the most important values for the success of Team Building environments runs contrary to human nature, and to most accepted management practices: *managing people for how well they serve their internal customers, instead of how well they perform their job functions.* This subtle but important distinction is perhaps the key reason that many team environments fail. This concept of internal customer relationships, when deployed throughout an organization, is one of the most powerful things you can do to ensure team success.

Rewarding people for how well they do their assigned jobs would seem to be the most natural thing in the world. It can also be one of the most dangerous. Let's say that your organization includes the following groups:

- A product development group that is rewarded for developing as many products as possible
- A sales and marketing group that is rewarded for selling as much as possible
- A shipping department that is rewarded for shipping as much as possible

What generally happens is that each department looks out for its own interests, to the detriment of the entire organization:

- Take, for example, the seemingly harmless goal of rewarding your shipping department for how much it ships. You've just encouraged them to create procedural hurdles that streamline their own productivity, at everyone else's expense. If you have ever been in an organization that requires forms in triplicate and several approval signatures before something is sent out, you have seen this phenomenon in action.
- Similarly, rewarding the product development group for just product quantity will lead them to shortchange product quality to meet their numbers. And sales and customer service issues become "interruptions" to the goal of making more product, hurting your revenues and service quality.
- Rewarding sales and marketing when they simply make quotas can lead to products being oversold to the wrong clients for short-term gain.

You can extend this analogy indefinitely in almost any business function. *You inevitably ruin performance by rewarding work group goals instead of global ones.* But with the internal customer model, the entire equation changes.

Let's take a look at what can happen in the same company when people are rewarded for managing internal customer relationships:

- The shipping department's job is now to serve the other departments, so they streamline the shipping process to where any department can electronically or physically have a shipment sent within seconds.
- The product development group is rewarded for both quality and product sales, so they welcome customer feedback and assist the sales effort. They plan for resources to serve sales and customer support efforts together with their development work.
- The sales and marketing department's mission is to build long-term customer relationships. They gather input from other departments, listen to customers and prospects, and become advocates for the future directions of the company. And ironically, they sell more than ever compared with the days of simply "moving product."

Internal customer relationships are a simple, powerful approach that helps organizational values transcend functional ones. Making them work requires cooperation at the management level and buy-in from the teams, because it isn't human nature to focus on the big picture instead of performing your functional job. But done well, these often become the catalysts for a great organization.

Perhaps the most significant aspect of the internal customer model is that it puts global, organizational goals in the hands of as many people as possible. In a sense, it promotes every person to a management role, because his or her job is to serve a business objective rather than just meet a quota or a deadline. Everyone becomes active participants in how to improve business processes, because they are focused on the ultimate goals rather than on the process itself. This represents one of the single most important ingredients in a Team Building culture.

WHY TEAMS FAIL

Employees at a major aerospace manufacturer once created a tongue-in-cheek flyer describing how an airplane looked to various groups in the company. For example, the power-plant group had a tiny airplane hooked up to two huge engines, the armaments groups had a plane that was mostly weapons, and the loft group (who designed the shape of the airplane) had two boards nailed together. It effectively poked fun at each group's radically different view of what was the most important thing on the aircraft.

Humor aside, many workplaces today have exactly the same perspective: we'll do our thing, and let others worry about their thing. For many workplaces, this eventually becomes a prescription for turf battles and low productivity. But for Team Building cultures who can see past this and work in a team environment, it represents a competitive advantage. With the right values and the right people, you can truly create a working environment where the whole is much greater than the sum of its parts.

This sense of "work group parochialism," and the tendency for it to become the natural order of things, is perhaps the biggest reason that work groups never become teams, even when they are called teams. This underlying atmosphere can lead to an environment that is in opposition to the needs of a team discussed previously, such as recruiting for aptitude, authority, responsibility, and proper management. From there, other more subtle factors can come into play that can sabotage the best intentions of a team, including:

- Putting the wrong people on a team
- Not understanding cultural and personality differences among team members
- Providing individual rewards and expecting team results
- Placing conflicting demands on team members
- Lacking goals that inspire a team to action

You could sum up all these common reasons for team failure by saying that many organizations don't realize that teams take work, as well as ongoing support. Moreover, people often misunderstand the reality of working in a team environment. People envision it as a utopia of camaraderie and mutual support, while in reality it is more like the dynamics of a family. Most teams, particularly good teams, are groups of highly committed people with different perspectives in pursuit of goals. This means that the team process is constantly evolving.

TEAMS ATTRACT STRONG PEOPLE— AND STRONG OPINIONS

I have been involved in numerous design teams during my career in the software industry, and to say that all was constantly sweetness and light would be less than candid. There are fundamental trade-offs in any software project: more features, a consistent design architecture, and a reachable project scope are all important goals that are by nature at odds with each other. Combine this with a group of people who are very talented and passionate about what they do, and it is not unusual to see disagreements erupt and even tempers flare at times. And yet, at the same time, most of these projects were highly successful in the end. It would be fair to characterize the vast majority of these design efforts as a constant process of education and negotiation, where the players involved ultimately walked away as friends.

The team approach seems like a natural virtue, but its successful implementation often requires the participants to behave contrary to human nature. Team traits such as autonomy, leadership, and responsibility for results require a level of trust that doesn't come naturally to most employer/ employee relationships. Yet in a very real sense, trust is the antidote to the human nature that pervades such relationships. It is far too common for most managers to revert to command-and-control and for employees to revert to PYA (protecting your analysis)—and in this all-too-human environment, teamwork cannot happen. But when you build trust among people, the energy spent controlling your people or defending yourself is instead directed to the good of the organization.

According to authors Diane Tracy and William Morin, the entire business world is evolving by necessity to a "coaching" style of management, one that revolves around seeking the truth and building trust—and you can't be a coach without a team. Succeeding in this quest for teamwork often means that your workplace becomes a family in both the good sense of the word (such as shared goals and effort) and the bad (such as frank opinions and conflicting passions). But like most good families, you also build a comfort zone where everyone ultimately pulls together for the best interests of the group, and creates bonds that cannot be easily broken. When you develop this trust, and make teamwork happen, you often gain a level of productivity and enthusiasm that would be hard to duplicate in any "normal" work group.

TEAMWORK AS A CULTURE

A good team workplace environment requires commitment and effort, starting from initial recruiting efforts, all the way to daily operations and long-term career planning. But the advantages are well worth the endeavor. For workplaces that successfully implement a Team Building environment, the benefits include higher productivity, greater levels of commitment, and better problem solving as a group. Most best-of-class organizations can ultimately point to a refined sense of teamwork as a cornerstone of their success.

A Team Building environment requires the right values. When management and employees don't trust each other, communication is poor, or workplaces suffer from departmental myopia, teams cannot happen no matter how much infrastructure you put behind them. The same goes for what kinds of people you bring into your organization, and their own fundamental values. To succeed in the long run, teamwork must go beyond a process or a program, to become an ingrained part of your culture.

Today, workplaces are more diverse and distributed than ever. Thanks to advances in telecommunications, computers, and network technology, it is not unusual to find your office watercooler spanning the nation, or the globe. This trend has accelerated the importance of a Team Building culture even further, and will continue to deepen the split in the marketplace between great cultures and lesser ones. In the future, the world will increasingly become our workplace—and as a result, the values of teamwork will ultimately be the glue that holds most great cultures' workforces together in the long haul.

Building Internal Customer Relationships

Southwest Airlines's Amazing Turnaround

Southwest Airlines has been a rarity in the airline industry: a consistently profitable low-fare air carrier with excellent on-time, safety, and customer service records. But for many years, its Web site contained a welcome message from former CEO Herb Kelleher that didn't say a word about missions, visions, or even customers. Instead, it was a short, plainly written message that centered around how Southwest "turns around" an aircraft from arrival to departure much more quickly than any of their competitors. It went on to say that this turnaround time is a big part of what enables the company to profitably offer low-cost, point-to-point air travel.

In point of fact, Southwest unloads and reloads an aircraft in an average of 20 minutes, nearly twice as fast as other major airlines, and this has a major impact on its costs and profitability. In their book *Nuts! Southwest Airlines' Crazy Recipe for Business and Personal Success,* authors Kevin and Jackie Freiberg point out that this short turnaround time translates to 35 fewer airplanes required to service Southwest's route system, and the resulting savings of more than $1 billion a year directly fuels their ability to serve as a low-fare airline. Perhaps the key to this amazing "turnaround" is strong team relationships between the people responsible for getting these planes back in the air.

In a sense, the simple act of turning around an aircraft in 20 minutes has become the cornerstone of an organization that, as of this writing, has become a $5 billion-plus company with more than 2,700 flights per day and more than 34,000 employees. From its beginnings in 1971 as a small start-up airline serving three Texas cities, it has now become the fourth-largest air carrier in the United States in terms of domestic customers. Behind this all is a company that has always stated, with no disrespect intended, that "the customer comes second"—and the people who come first at Southwest, the employees themselves, ultimately drive their company's success by serving each other.

At Southwest, there is actually no such thing as an employee. People who work for the giant air carrier are referred to as "internal customers," and they foster an environment where teams serve each other as well as the external customer. In a very real sense, one could say that Southwest's goal of a 20-minute turnaround helps foster many of these internal-customer relationships, and vice versa. When a Southwest plane lands, teams of people on the ground swarm over the plane, cleaning and restocking the aircraft, servicing the lavatories, loading bags, and getting the aircraft ready for departure. During this flurry of activity, it is not unusual to see gate supervisors helping out on the ramp, pilots walking through the cabin to cross seat belts, and even visiting senior management pitching in.

At a deeper level, Southwest actively encourages people to walk in each other's shoes and understand the functions of other jobs in the organization. Its "Cutting Edge" program gives people the opportunity to formally spend time doing other jobs—for example, a pilot may spend time working on the ramp or a customer-service agent may get involved in provisioning food and beverages for departing flights. Even outside the program, it's not unusual to see a Southwest pilot put on work clothes and load bags to help get a flight out. By trading places, people not only learn how other jobs work, but also develop a respect for the people doing them. Above all, experiences like this help people learn how to provide better internal service to other teams.

These internal customer relationships extend far beyond the obvious frontline functions that deal with getting customers and airplanes off the ground. For example, when faced with the need to acquire hundreds of personal computers for a new facility, most information technology (IT) departments would focus on simply justifying the expense. Southwest's IT department actually recruited fellow employees to assemble these computers from wholesale parts, saving the company more than $1 million. In turn, while Kelleher described himself as the "Aunt Maude" that technology needed to be simple enough for, he championed a cutting-edge environment for new technologies, including integrated flight-tracking systems and the first airline Web site on the Internet.

At a deeper level, this philosophy also means that the company can react quickly as a team when faced with external pressures such as competition or rising fuel prices. Pilots once decided to adopt a new flight regimen that used slightly less engine power during key phases of the flight, saving millions in fuel and engine wear. Similarly, Southwest quickly assembled an internal team of experts to become the first airline to offer electronic ticketing, when it became clear that other airlines would squeeze them out of their automated reservations and ticketing systems. And one time when another carrier launched a competing low-fare service on the West Coast, Southwest employees even came to work dressed in battle fatigues and greasepaint, ready to "go to war" with its bigger competitor.

Perhaps the internal culture at Southwest is best summed up in a message that was once posted to an online discussion group for airline professionals. In the middle of one discussion where several pilots were complaining about the working conditions and labor troubles at their various employers, one Southwest pilot posted a message saying that things were totally different at his carrier: groups such as its mechanics see pilots as their customers, have a great attitude, and do their best to serve them. And in turn, the pilots do things like host an annual barbecue for the mechanics. He went on to describe the culture at Southwest as utopia compared with his previous employers. (In fact, statistically, 5 percent of Southwest's employees are so fond of their coworkers that they married fellow employees.)

This dichotomy between operating efficiency and putting employees first has turned into a business model that has carried Southwest Airlines for more than 30 years. When customers think of Southwest, they think of an airline with no meals, no assigned seats, and the highest-rated customer service in the industry. When airline industry analysts look at Southwest, they see a carrier who taxies to the gate faster, hedges its fuel costs, and keeps a sharper eye on operating expenses than most carriers. And its employees are so dedicated to the airline that they voluntarily invest more than 70 percent of their profit-sharing funds in Southwest stock. The end result is a carrier that, according to *Fortune* magazine, had a market value greater than that of all other U.S. airlines combined in 2001—based around a unique culture that has never yet been duplicated.

5

The Nimble

Building an Infrastructure for Change

The Nimble are people who ban the phrase "we've always done things this way" from their vocabulary. They are the ones who see opportunity in change, whether it is in markets, technology, demographics, or other areas. Being Nimble is perhaps the most important long-term survival trait of any culture—it is the reason why IBM is no longer an adding machine company, Honda competes with automotive firms several times its size, and quite possibly the reason that your company will survive the trends of the next decade. Some traits they all share in common include the following:

We are willing to "bend the rules" to react quickly to competition. Once upon a time, purchasing new music was a gamble. You couldn't open and play albums in a store, and if you hadn't heard it first elsewhere, you were taking your chances. Then Amazon.com got the idea of using streaming audio technology to let customers preview music from almost any album on the Internet—and in the process, jumped from out of nowhere to become one of the world's largest music retailers.

We are ahead of similar firms in our use of technology. In the early days of the World Wide Web, Dell Computer once asked each of its employees to purchase a book online, to understand the impact that e-commerce would soon have on its own business. Today, nearly half of Dell's sales occur online, at lower transaction costs that continue to fuel its dominance of the personal computer market.

We spend more time analyzing customer trends than competitors do. Do you know how many people order steak on Tuesdays? Or what they call your customer-service center the most about? Or what trends in buying habits have emerged over the past year? Information is power, and today leading firms are capturing customer information, and using it at a more strategic level than ever before, to guide their current and future business plans.

This fundamental split between cultures that cling to tradition and Nimble ones that embrace the future has become even more critical in recent years, as change flies thicker and faster than ever in today's business environment. Corporate graveyards today are littered with the ones that were slow to adopt technology, the ones that never thought that Japan could build competitive electronics, the ones that never looked for talent past the old-boy network, and so on. Even companies that once enjoyed market leadership and public acclaim in their past have stumbled under the weight of internal or external change—and conversely, the "new economy" has given rise to a host of new success stories, whose fresh values mirror those of society itself. Ultimately, those cultures that stand the test of time do so because of fundamental values that serve organizations well in times of change.

HOW CULTURES EVOLVE—OR DEVOLVE

In the 1970s movie *Bananas,* comedian Woody Allen is part of a revolutionary South American guerrilla team that is out to topple a repressive government. The group succeeds in its mission, and almost immediately afterwards, the guerrilla commander starts issuing equally repressive edicts of his own, including "everyone must change their underwear every half hour." Similarly, the classic George Orwell novel *Animal Farm* details how a group of farm animals declares an egalitarian society, and then watches it evolve into a brutally totalitarian regime, bit by bit, as these freedoms become "inconvenient" for the stronger animals. In much the same way, time often leads to changes in business practices that can either reinforce a successful culture or sow the seeds of its ultimate downfall.

Change inevitably leads to new business processes, and in time, a new business culture. I once personally had a front-row seat for this phenomenon as part of a start-up software firm that eventually went public. In the early days of our existence, as a five-person operation, we were like an extended family in every good and bad sense of the word. We ate lunch together at Del Taco every single day, socialized together with our wives and families, argued about whose ideas were the best, and did everything from designing software architectures to loading and packing boxes as a group. But bit by bit, success changed our workplace. The first and most obvious change came when we all no longer fit in a single fast-food restaurant booth and stopped eating lunch as a group. A few months later came the first employee that was hired by an individual manager, without consulting the rest of the team. And in seemingly no time at all, our original team members were all in corner offices, with staff and schedules of our own—and we had to make appointments to see each other.

At the same time, what was even more fascinating was the growth of the entire industry we were in. In the California software industry of the 1980s, lots of small businesses like ours were finding success in the marketplace, and all of us were changing as we became bigger. Some of us became centers of innovation, others built strong customer relationships, while still others became rigid and bureaucratic. And *all* of us succeeded in the intervening years, fueled by the success of the industry itself. It was an exciting and crazy time analogous to the dot-com frenzy to come more than a decade later. However, the end result a few years later was predictable: Nimble environments that combined their products with responsiveness to their customers and the market have grown to become major corporations, while those that let their technology get ahead of these relationships are all—without exception—out of business today.

One unalterable fact is that if you grow, or even if you simply survive, you will change. This change often will come in the form of dozens or hundreds of individual decisions, the impact of which may be clear only in hindsight. Here are some guidelines for keeping a Nimble culture alive as it evolves.

Examine the Impact of New Processes

Workplace cultures rarely get worse because leaders wake up one morning and decide to make them so. More commonly, they start as a result of well-intentioned decisions that react to circumstances in daily business life.

Here is a minor example: Let's say that you run a small marketing firm and keep a refrigerator stocked with free sodas for employees. Over time, you double in size, and eventually notice a disproportionate increase in the cost of this soda—and then one evening, someone sees an employee carting cases of it into his personal vehicle. The employee is terminated and suddenly the free-soda policy is out the window. Before long, you start looking at other areas where employees could abuse your trust—and soon employees must start signing out office supplies from a locked cabinet, travel expenses are scrutinized with a fine-tooth comb, and managers have to approve any employee business expense.

Will your culture survive the loss of free sodas and a sign-out sheet for pencils? Perhaps. But if you don't see these things as part of a process, and examine where this process is headed, you will find that your culture is slowly but inexorably changing. You have certainly protected yourself from what has already happened, but in the process, you have added more processes and become less Nimble. Multiply this situation by all the things that go wrong in most businesses and you understand where human nature can ultimately lead them, and why being Nimble is a competitive advantage over them.

Ultimately, if you aren't careful with the impact of new business processes, you may find yourself in the same boat as a major oil company who hired one of my colleagues early in his career. Being left-handed, he wanted to switch his phone from one side of his desk to the other, necessitating a longer phone cord. First, he went to his management and was told that because it was a capital expenditure, approval by the company might take months. Next he proposed simply buying the cord for a few bucks himself and bringing it in. Sorry, they said, bringing in your own equipment was strictly against company policy for telecommunications equipment. Finally, he solved the problem for himself—he quit the company.

Examine the Impact of Growth

Nimble business cultures, of any size, are often inherently growth cultures. Dell Computer went from a college dorm room to the Fortune 500 in less than a decade and is now among its top 50 companies. Southwest Airlines is now the fifth-largest air carrier in the world, with 30,000 employees and nearly $6 billion in annual revenues, and is the *only* major carrier to be consistently profitable every year since the 1970s. Canadian restaurant chain St. Hubert parlayed spotless family dining and unfailing courtesy from a single chicken dinner restaurant to a 100-unit institution in Quebec and beyond. And the most successful small businesses in your town probably succeed far beyond their peers. No matter what size you are, growth is frequently a natural outcome of being Nimble.

Growth can be created and sustained by a culture unto itself, or even the concept of a culture. For example, a skeptical professor once gave FedEx CEO Fred Smith a low grade for his college paper proposing a nationwide hub-and-spoke package delivery system. But Smith pressed on, and his idea created a competitive multibillion-dollar industry that never existed before: the overnight delivery business. Conversely, forces in society can create sudden growth, such as the recent dot-com revolution, and then the underlying fundamentals of a business culture eventually drive who leads the industry and who falls from their overnight success. In either case, growth becomes a matter of core values and vice versa.

Growth is universally seen as a good thing. Yet an organization is most at risk when it is changing, and particularly when it is growing. As you add new people to your mix—whether it is a new midlevel manager or the acquisition of a new multibillion-dollar division—you change your culture. This means that the underlying philosophy behind who you hire, how you expand, and who leads you has a tremendous influence on what you will become in the future. How an organization handles the ramifications of growth is one of the more important factors in its long-term survival.

Examine Your Stance towards Change Itself

The late Gordon MacKenzie once likened many corporate cultures to a giant hairball. It starts small, but in the course of daily business life, as more rules and procedures are created, more hairs are added to it—and hairs are almost never taken away. His prescription was for individuals to "orbit" this hairball and not be totally sucked into it. But at a deeper cultural level, it is sometimes healthy to assess the state of your own corporate hairball, and see if it still reflects the current business reality you work in today, as one major airline once did with its own employee procedures.

PUTTING A MATCH TO THE OLD RULES AT CONTINENTAL AIRLINES

Back in the days that Continental Airlines struggled with poor service ratings and low morale, it had a nine-inch-thick manual of policies and procedures that had evolved over time. It eventually came to be known internally as the Thou Shalt Not book, because much of its content consisted of myriad rules about things that employees shouldn't or couldn't do. One day in 1995, around the start of Continental's dramatic turnaround under new CEO Gordon Bethune, upper management decided to drive home an unmistakable point about giving employees the authority to do what's right for the customer. They gathered a large group of employees together, put the Thou Shalt Not book in a 55-gallon drum, poured gasoline over it, and lit a match to burn it to a crisp.

Situations like this underscore how the biggest enemy of a Nimble business culture can sometimes be just the status quo itself. When things go wrong in a business, the instinctive human-nature response is to create yet another rule to deal with it, and before you know it, your own giant hairball is thick with policies and procedures. And when you try to change any of them, you are greeted with a firestorm of reasons why each rule is important, most based around whatever situation precipitated the rule in the first place. This raw change resistance is a major part of what holds many cultures back in the competitive marketplace, and particularly what makes some grow dysfunctional over time.

Few forces are more irresistible than the status quo. At either the corporate or the workplace level, change resistance is a force that keeps people and organizations from collaborating, modernizing, and improving. And even the best organizations must constantly be aware that status quo exists in their own operations. The most effective antidote for it is nurturing values that are bigger than the comfort zone of your current practices: organizations who focus on being leaders become willing to make changes that keep them ahead of the ones who focus on just getting by.

The simple fact is that human nature inexorably forces us towards more rules, more constraints, and less ability to change. It is why one history professor remarked that "when three or more people get together, the first thing they do is form a government." It is also why bureaucracies and corporations become hidebound in their own procedures over time. But the good news is that we all have control over whether this human nature continues to govern us in the future, and why entities ranging from the smallest firms to the largest governments can and do successfully reinvent themselves, with the right values in place.

THE INNER GAME OF CHANGE

Change is often influenced by what goes on around us: competitive pressures, new business models, and even broader changes in society itself. But being Nimble and open to change is a value that starts on the inside. It revolves around the ability to look at situations with a new set of eyes and question why everyone else has done things the ways they always have. When you master the inner game of change, possibilities often appear that didn't exist before for your competitors, such as in the following example of a major corporate call center based largely in spare bedrooms.

KEEPING AN AIRLINE RUNNING IN YOUR PAJAMAS

JetBlue is a relatively new low-fare air carrier, headquartered in New York City. But if you call its reservations center to book a flight, don't ask how the weather is in the Big Apple for most of its reservations agents work from their homes in Utah. The air carrier equips these home-based agents with computers, phone lines, headsets, and even pagers so that headquarters can keep in touch with them. More important, the company invested in simple-to-use reservations software that can be easily learned in one day versus the weeks of training often required for major airline reservation systems. And to keep their other skills and knowledge current, agents check in at regular intervals at JetBlue's call center in Salt Lake City. The result is highly motivated people, low real estate costs, and a flexible workforce that now handles nearly 20,000 calls per day.

Sometimes this inner relationship with change means looking for answers in places you wouldn't normally find them. Take the case, for example, of one software vendor who decided to improve its service quality with a very unusual new hire.

SHE'S ALMOST HUMAN

Log on to the Web site for software vendor **McAfee** and you will see a link to a "Site Assistant" who can answer your questions about McAfee products and services. Click on this link and an image of a woman appears with a chat screen next to it. She introduces herself as Lori, invites you to type in your questions, and quickly directs you to online resources that can answer them, often bringing up the appropriate Web page or download screen right in front of you.

Lori's manner is so friendly and helpful that male customers sometimes start asking personal questions to try to get to know her better. When this happens, she politely reminds them that she is there to provide professional assistance only. Which is a good thing for the people asking, because Lori isn't a person, she is a software program developed by a company called eGain, running on McAfee's Web site. Since implementing this technology, Lori now serves many of McAfee's average 600,000 daily site visitors at a fraction of the cost of its live customer-service agents, who also stand ready to help customers when needed.

Lori is not just an interesting technology or a great cost-cutting story, it is also a cultural metaphor for how businesses can respond to change. People have known for years that electronic transactions can cost much less than live ones. Some firms turn trends like this into ham-fisted approaches to reduce expenses at all costs, which is why many service operations hide behind "voice mail jail" and obtuse Web sites. But others look strategically at how they can use technology to improve their competitive position. In the case of McAfee's Lori, she was designed as a win-win situation on all sides. Customers are not forced to use her to get assistance, but she is there on McAfee's main Web page if needed. McAfee's own employees had feedback into her design and implementation, including how "friendly" her interaction with customers was. But perhaps most important, she was designed to provide better and richer content to customers than a live agent who may dispense information one word at a time to people over the telephone.

These are just some examples of the unique ways that Nimble cultures employ change to get and stay competitive. At a broader level, the key point is that adaptive cultures often champion finding new paradigms for business problems. They tend to look inside at their own goals and values, rather than just marching in lockstep with their competitors. And in many of these cultures, people feel that the very notion of competition itself is overrated.

COMPETITIVE ANALYSIS—A CONTRADICTION IN TERMS?

How do you beat your competition? According to W. Chan Kim and Renée Mauborgne, professors at the French business school INSEAD, one of the worst ways is by competing with them. In their study comparing high-growth firms against lesser performers, they found that firms who tried to benchmark and improve on their competition regressed towards their level, rather than dominating a market. The reason: your corporate efforts are all turned towards fueling a process that often only yields incremental improvement on what's already in the marketplace.

So, how do they feel the best way is to compete? Break the mold. They advise challenging your managers to dominate your market by questioning its basic assumptions and providing radically better value to customers. Their models of success are companies like Home Depot or Starbucks who create markets that never existed before versus, for example, consumer products manufacturers who keep adding features and end up with identically complex products.

Many cultures flounder in the myth of making products "better" versus fostering change and innovation. For example, Yahoo quickly became the first major Internet search engine in the 1990s by giving people a single place to find all the information the Internet had to offer. It filled a need that started when founders Jerry Yang and David Filo carried written lists of the 12 sites that once constituted the World Wide Web, while both were still Stanford graduate students. But as their company's fortunes blossomed, there were suddenly dozens of competing search engines that were "better"—perhaps having faster response times, searching in more places, categorizing the results, or even having the backing of major media networks. But not one of them became a serious competitor to Yahoo, which at one point had a market capitalization exceeding that of Kodak, because none could capture the mind-share of a clear "killer app" that got there first. On a personal note, I spent hundreds of hours researching corporate best practices for this project, using sources ranging from university libraries to proprietary business databases, as well as numerous Internet search tools. And what was usually my first choice among these search tools? You guessed it—Yahoo.com.

You may find useful information by researching what your competitors are doing, but you will only find your core values—and your basic mission—by looking in the mirror. This mission may involve doing existing things better than others, as IBM did when it created the IBM-PC to take personal computing beyond a market of hobbyists and students. Or it may involve breaking the mold entirely, as Yahoo did with its first Internet search engine. But either way, your long-term future is a product of choices that no outside market can make for you. And above all, they revolve around values that start from within.

THE OUTWARD VIEW OF THE WORLD

While your own personal choices determine your values, it is also important to be aware of the world around you, because it never stops changing. You and your culture do business in the public eye, within plain sight of a competitive landscape that never sleeps. And your customers themselves change over time. Thus, remaining Nimble means keeping aware of the world around you and your business, whether you are the smallest business or, as in the case that follows, one of the giants of the shipping industry.

FEDEX VERSUS UPS—SUCCESS BREEDS COMPETITION

FedEx became the darling of the business trade press for its corporate culture over many years, but at one point in the late 1990s it started losing market share to a suddenly more Nimble **UPS.** Why? Because of a dramatic shift in the marketplace. Retail commerce once revolved around shipping truckloads of one thing to bricks-and-mortar stores, but today, in the wake of the dot-com revolution, more and more of it entails individual boxes of things being shipped directly to consumers. UPS responded to this trend by taking a page from the FedEx playbook, creating its own air shipment hub in Louisville, and implementing its own tracking methodology. It went a step further by integrating this system with its massive fleet of residential delivery trucks. The uptake was a much cheaper shipping alternative for many firms, particularly in the business-to-consumer marketplace.

Of course, neither firm is sitting still today in what has become one of the hottest competitive markets in history for delivery services. The legendary FedEx culture still drives a corporation with more than $20 billion in annual revenues, behind the efforts of employees who "bleed purple" (the corporate color) for their company. Like the joke about old married couples starting to look alike as they grow older, however, FedEx's forays into ground shipping and UPS's inroads into overnight air delivery have created two opposing powerhouses who both continue to expand their respective market niches. And for at least one point in recent history, a firm known for dull brown trucks and upper management who once drove them was trading on the stock market at valuations similar to surging dot-com firms, and far beyond those of its rival FedEx, with its vaunted corporate culture.

Even in the best of circumstances, a strong corporate culture does not exempt a firm from the competitive pressures of the marketplace. And in the worst case, it can lead to a level of complacency that paralyzes change when it is needed. Successful cultures are particularly prone to a sense of organizational hubris, where they become blind to trends outside the organization. In time, this blindness can be crippling, or even fatal, as the market changes around them.

When most businesses first start up, they must listen closely to their customers—or die. But as time goes on, they can become all too comfortable listening to their own internal agenda and letting the voices of their customers fade into the background. For example, some friends of mine once chuckled at how a major Tex-Mex chain restaurant had the gall to move into their hometown of Albuquerque, New Mexico. As they explained, putting bland national restaurant fare into a city that was famous for award-winning Mexican cuisine was barely one step above starting an ice company in Alaska. They noted, with some relish, that the restaurant went out of business in short order.

Long-term survival in the marketplace requires both a keen sense of who you are and who your customers are. For instance, a dog obedience trainer once tried to market seminars on how to control a pet, and very few people showed up for them. One of his attendees, however, was a postal worker who was interested in learning how to avoid being attacked by dogs on his route. This led to a new focus on seminars about how to prevent dog attacks, and a vast audience suddenly appeared that included delivery personnel, police officers, utility workers, and other service professionals who had to work outdoors in residential neighborhoods. The trainer was able to eventually turn this new focus into a successful consulting and training practice.

This process of customers deciding who you are and where you go can often happen on a grand scale, and sometimes, there is more than a little irony in where you think you are going versus what your market teaches you.

AUTODESK—THE FLAGSHIP PRODUCT THAT NEVER EXISTED

As a small Sausalito, California, software start-up, **Autodesk** set out to tap the growing use of personal computers to automate the office desktop. Its flagship product, with the same name as the company, was designed to be a groundbreaking PC-based office management system. The firm's business plan also included several other independent applications, including AutoCAD, a small computer-aided design (CAD) program that also would run on PCs. Because many early computer users were engineers, this product mix of office automation and design products seemed like a good fit for the market.

To make a long story short, the Autodesk product itself never saw the light of day; its founders pulled the plug on it in the face of growing competition. AutoCAD, however, was a different story. As a $1,000 product that had many of the key functions of major CAD systems costing tens of thousands of dollars, it sold more than $1 million in its first year on the market—legitimizing not only the company, but also the concept of using personal computers for complex design tasks. Today, a company named after a product that never existed is now one of the world's largest software companies, with revenues in excess of $1 million a day.

Aside from learning the mind-set of your customers, you need to be true to who you are as well. Starbucks created an upscale image where it suddenly became fashionable to pay $3.50 for a latte instead of 75 cents for a cup of Joe. Its counter staff are known as *baristas,* and their stores reflect the culture of the young, hip, urban Seattle world that they came from. They eventually expanded to become a cultural institution—first to bookstores and urban centers, and later as far afield as major airlines and Pacific Rim nations. But in the process, they never sacrificed their core image of being a premium product for hip, well-to-do people. You would not find them in most factory cafeterias, nor, for many years, in Europe, which has long had its own style of coffeehouse culture. (As of this writing, however, Starbucks has recently tested the European market with an initial site in Vienna.) Overall, the company retains a customer base that resonates with who it is.

Being Nimble starts with an understanding of your market, a market that is constantly changing. From there, the decisions on when to lead, when to follow, and when to forge a new path are governed entirely by the internal compass of who you are and what your core values are. This process sometimes involves luck and timing, but it always involves a keen awareness of both yourself and the outside world. Combined with the underlying culture that your organization brings to the table, this awareness becomes a key factor in whether you control your market or it controls you.

UNDERSTANDING CHANGE AND CULTURE

Your adaptability to change—in other words, how Nimble you are—is perhaps the ultimate measure of the strength of your business culture. It is what eventually separates fads in the marketplace from businesses with lasting value—from businesses ranging from 1970s disco Studio 54 to the firms behind the recent millennial scooter craze. True success is always measured in the long term, and more often than not it combines ongoing business fortunes with deeper core values.

At the same time, sustaining a Nimble culture in the face of change serves as the market's validation of a successful business, and surviving its challenges establishes a pattern for your long-term success. How you manage the three key aspects of your relationship with change—your culture's evolution, your inner relationship with change, and your view of the outside world—not only determines your level of success, but helps define "who you are" as an organization long into the future. When these things are done well, in the right business environment, change management ultimately moves from being a challenge unto itself to becoming an integral part of your own business culture.

Change can be a powerful force in any business, and this power can be harnessed for the good of the organization—or serve as a force that magnifies your weaknesses and sows the seeds of later decline. How it is managed can be more powerful than any external market force, and your relationship with it ultimately defines you.

AutoNation

If at First You Don't Succeed, Expand Again

Autonation wasn't simply a great idea in auto retailing. It was, in fact, two or three great ideas that were tried in succession, and the lessons learned from them helped eventually propel this dealer network to its current position on the Fortune 100. Today, it is the nation's largest automotive retailer, selling more than 500,000 cars per year across a network of dealerships from coast-to-coast. On an average business day, someone purchases an automobile from one of AutoNation's dealerships every 20 seconds.

Founder Wayne Huizinga was experienced in going into markets in a big way, having previously built Waste Management and Blockbuster Video from small regional operations into national market leaders. With Auto-Nation, his initial idea was to create a chain of used-car superstores across the United States. Within a few years, AutoNation outlets dotted locations across the country, featuring acres of preowned vehicles, fixed no-haggle prices, and polite, salaried sales consultants on golf carts ready to help buyers find whatever kind of vehicle they were looking for.

AutoNation's parent company also expanded into the car rental business, acquiring National Car Rental, Alamo Rent-A-Car, and CarTemps. In addition, it began acquiring new-car dealerships as well as service providers such as financing operations. It seemed like a natural fit—new cars could be leased to customers, returned and put into rental service, then sold or leased back to customers again through AutoNation used-car centers. This pipeline of inventory was designed as the linchpin of a nationwide system that would reduce costs and set a new competitive benchmark for automotive sales and leasing.

It was a plan designed to create a full spectrum of automotive sales and services on a grand scale never before implemented. Unfortunately, it turned out to be too grand in the eyes of both the marketplace and the stock market. By the end of the decade, the used-car superstores were shuttered or converted to new-car dealerships, and the rental car operations were spun off into a separate corporation. These moves boosted revenue per AutoNation employee over 80 percent, leading it to the highest productivity gains of any major corporation over the past half of the 1990s decade. More important, this transition sowed the seeds of its current and most successful corporate identity—the largest network of new-car retailers in the United States.

Today, AutoNation has expanded to a network of nearly 400 dealerships, focusing in the process on the most profitable segment of its former business model. Within this market, its growth has driven three key competitive advantages for these dealers:

1. *Economies of scale.* By functioning under a common corporate umbrella, AutoNation can tap into an inventory of more than 100,000 cars at any given time, as well as develop common standards for areas such as service and maintenance. And by consolidating back-office operations, it achieves costs savings and profit margins that would otherwise be impossible for individual dealerships to achieve on their own.

2. *Changing the customer experience.* For many people, the car-buying experience has been about as much fun as having a root canal, and the business as a whole has long had a black eye from consumers' experiences with traditional automotive salespeople. AutoNation has leveraged this dissatisfaction to create a consistent low-pressure sales

experience, together with a three-day, 150-mile money-back guarantee, "fast or free" guarantees on routine maintenance, and uniform warranties on used vehicles.

3. *Tapping into the Internet.* Cyberspace has become a prime medium for car buyers nowadays, with a substantial percentage of customers doing at least some research on the Net. As a result, part of Auto-Nation's strategy has been to dominate the Internet. In the process, it has created one of the most hassle-free car-buying experiences in cyberspace. Firm e-mail price quotes and vehicle information are available on demand, with the ball always in the customer's court to proceed further with the dealership. Other online tools include vehicle comparisons, third-party reviews, and even a calculator for the value of your trade-in. And unlike other third-party Internet car-buying services, AutoNation's Internet sites serve as cost-effective means of generating sales leads, rather than as added transaction costs. As a result, AutoNation has become the nation's largest automotive retailer on the Net as well as off it.

Changing an entrenched and highly fragmented industry is never easy, and AutoNation has chosen a strategy of growth and consolidation within a business that does not always welcome empire builders. Automotive manufacturers, for example, have at times clashed with the company over naming and dealer acquisition issues, not wanting a unified national dealer brand drowning out loyalty to their own brands. For this reason, AutoNation dealerships still carry local and regional names rather than the corporate one. Similarly, the no-haggle pricing policies that once were a cornerstone of its used-car superstores haven't translated well to the national retail marketplace because of competitive undercutting. But growth by expansion remains the engine that drives AutoNation and its business model for the long term.

Today, AutoNation has annual revenues of about $20 billion per year, and in the midst of a recession, its shares have recently outperformed the Standard & Poor's 500 by more than 20 percent. In 2002, it topped *Fortune* magazine's list of Most Admired Companies in the automotive market segment. As for the future, CEO Mike Jackson, a former automotive technician and "car guy" who previously headed Mercedes's U.S. operations, states that "AutoNation aims to become America's best-run and most profitable automotive retailer." In the meantime, it serves as a good example of how a business evolved through successive expansion models and eventually emerged to lead its industry.

6

The Customer Champions
Building a Service Culture

Customer Champions are the ones who realize that certain core values determine what really happens in the individual "moments of truth" that every business has with its customers. They see customers not just as people who should be treated well, but as strategic partners with whom to build long-term relationships. By building their business strategies around this principle, Customer Champions breed the kind of customers who, in turn, make their organizations successful. You could summarize their beliefs as follows:

We feel that excellent customer service is primarily a process. Some companies view customer service as synonymous with "smile training," while others, like insurance giant USAA, start each new employee off with a weeklong orientation about its culture and business practices. Similarly, many successful restaurant chains deliver consistent service by publishing internal standards for practices such as greeting, closing, check and change processing, and problem resolution. If you scratch the surface of most consistently high-service organizations, you will find clear training and operating methodologies behind them.

We benchmark our processes by being "customers" ourselves. In the early days of Motown Records in the 1960s, its staff would gather to listen to potential new releases on a cheap record player, to hear them the same way many customers would. Afterwards, the decision to release a record hinged on one question: "If you were down to your last dollar, would you buy this record or a sandwich?" Today, leading companies still work hard to benchmark the customer experience, putting them ahead of competitors who would be surprised at what they might discover if they ate at their own restaurants, shopped at their own stores, or flew their own airlines.

We capture data about customer transactions and react to it strategically. Most leading organizations treat the opinions of their customers like pure gold, because in a very real, financial sense, it is. In today's competitive environment, businesses of any size must measure and track their level of customer satisfaction and analyze the reasons behind it. Truly customer-driven companies keep a regular "pulse" of their service quality and use the results to drive their operations.

As customers ourselves, most of us tend to have a simplistic view of customer service: good organizations provide good service, and bad ones provide bad service. In reality, however, most service cultures aren't that simple. As with other business factors, they are created by well-intentioned decisions—usually from the top—that ultimately determine the course of their interactions with customers.

This means that bad service often has its roots in situations where legitimate concerns, such as costs, returns, or inefficiency, lead to policies and practices that ultimately create an atmosphere of disrespect for the customer, the employee, or both. Conversely, great service is usually the product of deeper underlying values, which lead to intentional choices that drive your daily workplace operations. In either case, a company's basic stance towards its customers is perhaps the most visible aspect of its culture.

The impact of Customer Champions on an organization can be dramatic. For example, firms with high customer satisfaction scores have been shown to spend 40 percent less on marketing, retain customers for twice as long, and in some cases nearly double their profitability. According to a Wharton study in the mid-1990s, companies with measurably strong service cultures outperform their peers on the stock market by 25 percent. And for Customer Champions, excellent service goes far beyond good customer relations and becomes a way of life, as is the case at one of the world's premier hotel chains.

RITZ-CARLTON—A SYSTEM BEHIND BEST-OF-CLASS SERVICE QUALITY

The Ritz-Carlton hotel chain has become justifiably famous for its service quality, both among customers and the business trade press. Ritz-Carlton guests are served by employees who seek out and cater to guest preferences, go above and beyond the call of duty to accommodate requests, and deliver a highly personalized service experience. In a recent example, when one Ritz-Carlton guest in Atlanta asked about locating a specialty grocery store, the staff looked up the address for her, and when they discovered there was no convenient ground transportation there, they arranged for the bellman to drive the guest there.

Unlike most hotel chains, where customer service is addressed via training programs or incentives, there is a great deal of infrastructure behind Ritz-Carlton's approach to service. For example, employees carry "guest preference pads" where they note customer requests for later entry into guest databases—if you request a soft pillow in Boston, you will find another one waiting for you in Osaka, Japan. Each employee is financially empowered to make situations right for guests, up to a substantial dollar limit. Most important, the chain fosters a culture where even the most humble frontline employee is treated with as equal respect as senior management.

While every organization states that it is in favor of good service, market leadership and success overwhelmingly belong to those who make a culture of service one of their deep, underlying values. In an emotional town-hall meeting with employees following the September 11, 2001, tragedy, where the American Express Company was displaced from its headquarters and lost 11 employees, chairman and CEO Kenneth Chenault said, "There is no higher purpose in life than serving people, and if I am going to be in a business that generates revenues and makes profits, I am proud to be in one that makes all its revenue from serving other people. And this is why we shall overcome." Perhaps a broader way to express this sentiment is that great service quality does not define a culture; rather, a great culture defines its service quality.

BUSINESS CULTURE AND YOUR CUSTOMERS

Because no business exists without customers, most logical people would think that every workplace would be in favor of good customer service—like being in favor of apple pie and motherhood, particularly in today's economy. However, the experience that most of us have as customers is often very different from the ideal, as was my experience in the following situation.

SORRY, WE'RE TOO BUSY TO TELL YOU YOUR GRANDMOTHER DIED

Word came to me late one evening that my grandmother was dying in a New York area hospital. After a fitful night, I called the hospital the next morning to check on her condition and a curt, unpleasant woman snarled, "Nobody here by that name." I started to say, "She was there last night, and . . ." when I was cut off with, "I'm telling you, there's no one here by that name. Good-bye."

A couple of minutes later, I composed myself and called back, and got the same person. I started to explain, "My grandmother, Estelle . . ." when I was cut off again with, "I thought I just told you she's not here." Finally, I was able to blurt out that I thought she had died last night. Without missing a beat, she retorted, "Well, what building was she in?" Fortunately, I happened to remember this information, and was eventually transferred to a nurse who gave me the news that she had indeed passed away overnight.

Undoubtedly this hospital has mission statements, vision statements, and advertising that talks about health and wellness. But it also has a corporate culture that tolerates treating people very rudely in difficult situations. And in all likelihood, its upper management probably has no idea why its occupancy rates, customer satisfaction levels, and operating revenues are not what they should be, or could be.

Culture also governs an organization's response to a problem. What if I had written this hospital to complain about an incident like this? There would probably be a reprimand, a notation in the woman's personnel file, and with enough incidents, she might perhaps be fired. At a very real level, however, this situation probably goes deeper than this woman's behavior. The real problem is more likely with the people who hired her and oversee her work—more important, with a system that tolerates these customer experiences or even misses their existence entirely. Many factors come into play at moments like these, ranging from how much information the receptionist has access to, to how much importance her employers place on her position.

Let's take this problem a level deeper. Suppose that I were to confront this woman's direct supervisors personally about my service experience. How would they respond? In all likelihood, you would hear statements like:

- You can never find any good help nowadays.
- You can't control employees' attitudes anymore.
- It's much tougher work in health care today.

And meanwhile, if this receptionist were out for a couple of beers some night with her friends, what kinds of things would she say about her employer? Perhaps things like:

- She works for indifferent people who are always cutting costs.
- People increase her responsibilities without even asking her first.
- Managers don't spend much time with her other than to criticize something.

This is where the unspoken nature of an organization's culture comes in. It permeates several "moments of truth" that, in sum total, almost predetermine how situations like mine will eventually be handled. Do you give in to the pressure of hiring a warm body rather than waiting for the right person? How much time to you spend training a new employee? Is there any ongoing interest or coaching in the employee's daily performance? Does he or she feel like part of a team, or is he or she simply told what to do? Perhaps most important, do you have a gut sense of "who we are" and use that sense to guide all your daily decision points?

It is not as though hospitals and health care organizations do not care about their service quality anymore. In fact, most are under substantial competitive pressures nowadays to improve customer satisfaction. Speak with almost any hospital administrator nowadays and you are likely to hear about "improving their Press Ganey scores," referring to a survey widely used in the industry as an objective measure of service quality. Good versus poor Press Ganey scores can represent an important difference in the marketplace. Some hospitals, however, may respond to low scores by ordering up frantic rounds of customer-service training, while never looking at the underlying sense of "who we are." As a result, these efforts often are doomed to failure. Conversely, Customer Champions develop a strong service culture that often becomes self-policing and self-perpetuating, as with the case of one of the nation's leading hospitals.

MASSACHUSETTS GENERAL HOSPITAL— EXCELLENCE AS THE SUM OF ITS PARTS

At Massachusetts General Hospital, consistently one of the top-ranked hospitals in the nation for service quality, success isn't created by a single overall service initiative. Nor is it defined solely by its high quality of medical expertise, as the main teaching hospital for Harvard Medical School. Rather, it is defined by specific efforts by each individual department to define itself as the best in its field. For example, its medical staff recently pioneered an ambitious telemedicine initiative that takes its specialists to remote villages in Cambodia, its food and nutrition department became the first nonrestaurant to win the state's Best Restauranteur of the Year award, and even its maintenance department is a leader in areas such as integrated pest management and online facilities information.

As of this writing, Mass General ranks among the top three hospitals in the nation according to *U.S. News and World Report*'s rankings, and was recently one of just three hospitals to receive the national Customer Service Excellence Award from the University Healthcare Consortium. From its beginnings in the 1800s, when it was the first hospital in the United States to use developments such as anesthesia and X-rays, to today's cutting edge research in areas like transplantation and cancer research, it has made a conscious decision to maintain a service culture that matches its clinical reputation.

So what do stories like these mean to your own work group and its service culture? First, it means that good service starts long before your business interacts with its customers, in the way that you see yourselves and your employees. Second, it means that service quality isn't the exclusive domain of a customer-service department. It touches every corner of your business, in the same way that Massachusetts General Hospital sees how food, computer technology, and even janitorial services become part of a world-class reputation for medical care. Finally, more subtly excellent service starts with a genuine sense of pride within the workplace.

Lessons such as these show why bad service often can't be fixed by simply ordering up more customer-service training, and why excellent service may be as close as developing a consistent, organization-wide system of values. Customer Champions have a system behind their service, based on these values, that everyone in the organization is on board with. If you look at the mechanics of great service cultures, you can generally break down their success into three core components:

1. Executing the fundamentals
2. Seeing the world through your customers' eyes
3. Getting your policies and your service culture in harmony

The mechanics behind these three components are what differentiate cultures of great service from cultures of human nature. And if you examine the operations of most businesses that provide consistent, measurable service quality, you will see clear similarities that cluster around these three areas. Understand them and you will see, perhaps for the first time, why excellent service goes far beyond just teaching people how to smile.

EXECUTING THE FUNDAMENTALS

Many people view customer service as a matter of attitude, and much of what passes for customer-service training nowadays focuses on exhorting people to have a "good attitude." Common courtesy and the right attitude are indeed essential to good service. But if you look critically at Customer Champions who provide consistently excellent customer service, you will find that it is as much a matter of execution as it is of attitude. Compare the following two scenarios and you will understand how service and execution follow each other:

- You call a customer-service center about getting a broken product fixed and are told in a monotone that you have to first mail it copies of your receipt, your warranty from the product manual, and the original packing list, and then the center will get back to you sometime in the next two weeks about how to proceed from there. You insist that you need this product fixed much sooner than that and the person responds, "Sorry, that's policy."
- You bring in your car for a warranty repair and you are greeted and told exactly what time the work will be finished. When you return to pick the car up later that same day, it has been freshly washed and vacuumed, and there is hot coffee and pastries waiting for you in the lobby of the service department. A day later, someone from the dealership calls you to see if everything was fixed to your satisfaction.

Now what do you think would happen if the person at the first customer-service center attended a daylong course on how to be "nice"? *It would not change the underlying culture that caused him or her to be uninspired, and you to be dissatisfied, in the first place.* Likewise, in the second situation, your satisfaction went far beyond people being trained to smile and act polite. Things worked because someone thought through the fundamentals of the company's service process ahead of time and executed them.

Even in many situations that seem to be matters of simple rudeness, there are often more basic cultural reasons why people don't get the service experience they deserve. These generally involve areas such as how much authority people have, how much information they have access to, and what they are rewarded (or punished) for on the job. While individual attitudes are certainly important, the root causes of service quality often go far deeper than that. Here are some of the more visible factors in how Customer Champions "execute" a good service experience.

A Public Commitment to Service

What you say to your customers about service is very important. What you say to your employees is even more important. And how you act when making a great service choice might inconvenience you, cost you money, or delay your production is perhaps the highest public statement of all. Getting service on everyone's agenda and then walking the talk in your daily business decisions is perhaps the most important first step in becoming a Customer Champion. For example, when Lillian Vernon decided to use service as a differentiating factor in the catalog industry, the result was a corporate empire.

NO TIME LIMIT ON SATISFACTION

When Lillian Vernon created the catalog company that bears her name in 1951, she entered a mail-order business that was often known for shoddy products and little consumer recourse. To differentiate herself from the rest of the pack, she publicized a no-questions-asked, money-back guarantee, and combined it with the unusual policy of having no time limit—ever—for returns. Today, it continues to flourish as a quarter-billion-dollar-per-year operation.

One day, her company received a package of dishware from a woman in England. She had ordered it 20 years ago, never opened the box, and now decided that she didn't need it. The company had to conduct quite a bit of research to find out what they were selling 20 years ago and how much it cost, but the woman received her refund.

This ability to make a public service commitment and adhere to it is what ultimately separates a Customer Champion from a service slogan. This commitment is what drives employees behavior around customers in the trenches, and how these employees in turn are treated behind the scenes. It simplifies a great many cases of situational ethics into a common set of values, internally and externally.

Published Service Standards

Ten minutes or less, guaranteed. Help whenever you need it. Satisfaction or your money back. These are all examples of taking a service concept and defining your culture around it. Even when your own service standards aren't destined to become corporate slogans, making service standards public is an important statement to both your customers and your team, even when you are one of the world's largest governments.

GOOD SERVICE FROM BIG GOVERNMENT? BELIEVE IT

A decade ago, government bureaucracies would have seemed like the least likely candidates for service leadership. But thanks to well-publicized service improvement initiatives in the United States, United Kingdom, and elsewhere, many government agencies now meet standards for service and response that actually exceed those found in private industry, and they have accomplished this during a period of major downsizing in government.

The **Social Security Administration,** for example, that at one time had less than 60 percent of its callers get through on the first try, set a service standard of having 95 percent of its callers reach the service within five minutes. By investing in sophisticated call-routing equipment and cross-training employees outside its call centers to take calls during peak periods, it has now met that goal every year since 1997. Similarly, the UK's Service First initiative set standards such as acknowledging all letters within two days, responding to issues within one to two weeks, and meeting in-person appointments within ten minutes of scheduled times. In the year 2000, it met these standards for 98 percent of its mail and 100 percent of its appointments.

The internal side of these service standards cannot be overlooked, either. Overall job satisfaction among federal employees is now comparable to that of the private sector, and a majority feel that their agencies have truly improved their levels of customer service. More important, the public is now receiving the same level of responsiveness from many public agencies that was once reserved for profit-making industries. Successes like these serve as powerful lessons for how service standards themselves can become cultural change agents.

Coaching and Training on the Mechanics

Good customer skills are not the same thing as simple courtesy. They are professional skills that need to be learned and practiced. Knowing how to communicate when someone has a problem, how to defuse an angry situation, or how to gracefully take control of a transaction all involve techniques that go far beyond human nature. Customer Champions have systems in place to train, coach, and mentor people as they learn to reflect the style of the organization. These systems can make a substantial difference in what happens on the front line, as I recently demonstrated at a major university.

THE MESSENGER IS AS IMPORTANT AS THE MESSAGE

I once taught a customer skills seminar for the payroll department at Cornell University to help prepare its employees for implementing a brand-new online payroll system. Knowing that they might be getting calls from people who had problems with their paychecks, I had students in the class role-play speaking with an angry person whose check was late. At first, they were all frozen like deer in the headlights, muttering things like, "I'm sorry sir, you'll just have to wait."

Next, I explained about how a customer's anger depended as much on one's communications technique as the situation itself, and taught them a structured technique known as "staging" designed to respond to bad news. This was a three-step process in which they would address the issue in stages, as follows:

1. Summarize the problem.

2. Explain the issues.

3. Empathize with every feeling the customer expresses.

With staging, people found themselves instead saying things like, "I can see that your paycheck should have come out on schedule, and I'd really like to apologize for that. Because running a new check is a two-day process, I am going to personally make sure that we run this tomorrow, and we have a check waiting for you the first thing Thursday. Will this work for you?"

The people in the class did learn how to communicate better. But what was even more amazing was to watch the lights go on in people's heads, as they all realized that the complaining person *could not stay angry* when they used these techniques. One person joked, "I could practically tell people that their cars are being towed away, as long as I do it the right way." And they learned that, with practice, their ability to deliver a great service experience was not just at the mercy of the situation itself.

At the same time, implementing a coaching program is fraught with peril without the right values reinforcing it. How you administer your coaching procedures makes all the difference in how well you succeed. For example, how often have you called for service, heard a recorded message that "this call is being monitored for coaching purposes," and then spoken to a bored, indifferent service representative? The experience may say something about the person on the phone, but it speaks volumes about the people who manage him or her. Customer Champions who employ supportive coaching to help people become great at what they do obtain a very different outcome than people who monitor, track, and punish every little mistake.

Strong Complaint Resolution Procedures

For many businesses, where service succeeds or fails lies in how they handle problems when they arise. Right here, in the zone where a customer's complaint may cost money or cause inconvenience, is where core values separate organizations that say they have good service from those who walk the talk. Examples like the one that follows from Nordstrom show how Customer Champions leverage this principle to lead their markets.

NORDSTROM WANTS YOU TO BE SATISFIED ONLINE OR OFF-LINE

Upscale clothing retailer Nordstrom is well known for its flexible return policy. There is even a widespread story that it once gave a refund to a customer who rolled in a pair of tires, which the store does not sell. (There is more to this story than meets the eye, for Nordstrom had reputedly just purchased this store from a chain that did sell tires. However, the incident remains part of company lore.) At the same time, the company is indeed famous for painlessly accepting returns on any of its merchandise, with no need for sales slips and no questions asked. Nordstrom clerks have even been known to go to other stores to purchase replacement merchandise that is not stocked at their own store.

Today, in the e-commerce era, Nordstrom uses this same return philosophy to its competitive advantage. In a world where many Web shopping sites entomb their return information in far corners of their site, Nordstrom's return and exchange information is front and center on its home page. It is also one of few online retailers who saves its customers a trip to the post office for returns, sending them a prepaid envelope for pickup or allowing them to return items to a regular Nordstrom store. You can even print your return shipping label online directly from its Web site.

Complaint resolution can be a complex issue, particularly in the retail sector. When profit margins are thin, an abundance of returns can seriously impact the bottom line, and some major chains in areas such as consumer electronics and computers have cited high returns as a factor in their business failures. It is also an area where large businesses often have an advantage over small businesses, who often feel that they lack the financial ability to absorb a major return or provide extensive recompense. It is here, where providing a good service experience can run counter to financial goals, where the rubber of service quality meets the road.

These procedures also serve as defining moments in the level of trust between you and your customers. If you speak with almost any career retail professional, you will hear stories of how customers try to "beat the system"—for example, returning an expensive formal dress right after a party or wearing a pair of sneakers for several months and then claiming they are defective. At the same time, retailers such as Wal-Mart combine a liberal return policy with strong logistics and profit margins, and others such as Lands' End or L.L. Bean leverage a good service reputation to command premium prices that support a generous lifetime return policy. These firms, in turn, raise the service bar for everyone else in the industry.

Each of these factors are fundamental to great service. They are factors you can control, which, in turn, influence the more intangible results of service quality. More important, each can become a defining part of your culture. A business that is as obsessive about returns as Nordstrom is is primed to make customer transactions happy ones. A service standard can become a microcosm of the teamwork needed to make it happen. And a well-trained workforce learns how to handle any situation with class, and develops professional pride in their skills. Great service starts with skills and policies, and ultimately turns into a facet of your culture.

SEEING THE WORLD THROUGH YOUR CUSTOMERS' EYES

Human beings—and organizations—have an amazing ability to shift perspective. One minute you are driving a car, wishing these slow, lazy pedestrians would get out of your way. The next minute you are walking across the street, wishing these reckless drivers would slow down and be more careful as you cross. These same phenomena drive a great many organizational service failures, and understanding them can become a key competitive advantage for businesses of any size.

As individuals, we all are acutely aware of what it's like to be a customer. In a corporate setting, however, this perspective can shift rapidly. People focus on their jobs instead of on their ultimate consumers, and customers become interruptions, statistics, and costs to be reduced wherever possible. Ultimately, employees and managers alike can easily lose sight of how each of them affects the big picture that the customer sees, as a colleague of mine recently experienced at his local auto dealership.

GO AWAY, IT'S OUR LUNCH HOUR

One day, a colleague of mine took his car in over his lunch hour to a dealer for repairs, just before heading off on a business trip. He drove around to the service department, pulled in, and waited—and waited. Finally, after no one came over, he got out of his car, walked into the garage towards the mechanics, until one of them yelled, "Hey, buddy, you're not supposed to be in here."

As he retreated towards his car, someone finally appeared munching from a bag of fast-food french fries. With his mouth still full, this person muttered, "We're closed during lunch hour. You'll have to come back." Because my friend had a plane to catch, he finally went into the dealership's sales floor and asked a salesperson if he would check the car in for service when the dealership reopened. "Uh, yeah, I guess so." was the response.

A day later, by now halfway across the country, he called the dealership to check on the status of his car and was greeted with "Who are you? Sorry, we don't have any record of your car being brought in for service." It ultimately took a lot of angry phone discussions to finally motivate this dealer to locate and fix my colleague's car.

So what went wrong here? Aside from having a supremely bad attitude, the seeds of service failure were probably sown by this dealership long before my friend pulled into the lot. First, it starts with the logistics:

- A nonstandard policy for service hours
- No process for handling lunch hour service dropoffs
- Mechanics who yell at customers instead of helping them
- A poorly trained and motivated sales staff
- Employees eating in front of customers
- *Et cetera*

Then there are more strategic issues. How well does this dealership know its market? Does it realize that customers are often more free to bring in cars over their lunch hours? Has it ever looked critically at the impact of having a "that's not my job" culture? Its service quality may ultimately have less to do with courtesy and more to do with questions it never asked about the whole customer experience. Perhaps, it lost sight of what it is like to be one of its own customers.

Customer Champions regularly benchmark the entire customer experience, as seen through the customers' eyes. Here as well, doing this consistently is not simply an attitude but a set of underlying best practices that spring from core values.

Be Your Own Customer

Many business processes are developed around your own team's ideas about what it is like to be the customer. Still other processes are created in reaction to internal concerns and, unwittingly or not, don't consider the customer at all. In either case, until you benchmark these business processes through the eyes of your customers, you are missing an important quality assurance step that holds these new ideas up against the reality of your customers' experience.

Becoming your own customer means walking through your own business the same way that a consumer would. It means eating at your own restaurants, contacting your own call centers, and shopping at your own stores. And above all, it involves a focus towards process benchmarking and process improvement. For example, while some retailers may use outside mystery shoppers to simply catch employees providing good and bad service, the best ones go a step further and examine the mechanics of the whole customer experience—such as the greeting, closing, wait times, and even the layout and merchandise mix of the store itself.

Solicit Customer Feedback and Measure Customer Satisfaction

Customer-satisfaction surveys have been a ubiquitous part of the consumer landscape for some time, ranging from one restaurant chain's simple yes/no question "I'll be back" to a six-page online survey sent by a major software firm to its technical support callers. Today "customer sat," as it is known in the industry, has become more important than ever. In today's automated environment, levels of customer satisfaction can provide more feedback than ever before, ranging from how people liked today's meal to trends that drive where you should build your next hotel.

At the same time, many companies often make one of three fatal mistakes when measuring customer satisfaction:

1. One is to measure what *you* think is important rather than what the *customer* thinks is important. Companies who lose market share despite acceptable customer-satisfaction ratings often fall victim to not getting their customers on the front end of the assessment process.

2. Another is to use ranking-style questions only, where customers rate you from one to five or poor to excellent. Open-ended questions represent an important window into customers' minds and allow them to share feelings that aren't covered in your questions. The best questions are ones that do not allow a simple yes or no answer: if you ask someone, "How was your meal?" the answer will invariably be "fine," but a question like "What areas could we most improve?" will lead to a wellspring of feedback.

3. The third mistake is to not turn your ratings into an action plan. There is a fallacy among many companies that "good" or "average" ratings are no cause for concern. Nothing could be further from the truth. According to a 1996 Xerox study, customers who rank you a four out of five in surveys are six times more likely to leave you than those who give you a five. This is because any less-than-perfect score means that the customer is holding something back and is less than satisfied in at least some tangible way. And of course, any less-than-satisfactory score should be a strong signal to follow up with the customer and resolve the problem.

On the other hand, customer-satisfaction measurement remains one of the most powerful tools for seeing the world through your customers' eyes, and then using this data to build a better customer world. By using customer input to design your survey tools, leaving room for open feedback, and acting aggressively on the results, you can quickly start aligning your operations with what the customer sees.

Blending Your Internal and External Customer Relationships

Customers often view service as an interaction between themselves and another person. In reality, often a number of interconnected relationships are needed for a good service experience to happen. And when these relationships do not work in harmony, the results can be disastrous.

LET'S CLOSE EACH OTHER'S EXITS

In one large northeastern city, the state highway department was involved in a major construction project. It would close freeway interchanges at regular intervals and divert traffic onto other thoroughfares. One morning, the city public works department came to repair a road and diverted traffic to one exit, not realizing that the state had closed *that* exit to do its own repairs. After both departments effectively closed each other's detours at the height of rush hour, this city became a parking lot for much of the morning.

As discussed in an earlier chapter, an important part of seeing the world like a customer lies in analyzing the internal relationships that lead to that customer experience. A good example is the relationship between the servers who take orders in a food-service operation and the back-of-house staff who prepare and deliver the food. Helping groups like these work together as a team has a strong impact on morale, execution, and other factors that ultimately drive the service experience.

A more subtle point behind internal customer relationships is that to make them work, your values and reward structure must often move from production benchmarks to service ones. Most people genuinely try to do what their employers expect, and rewarding people to serve other teams instead of blindly reaching productivity goals represents a critical turning point for many businesses. When you expand this concept to all your business activities, you will learn that creating a culture of good *customer* service ultimately goes hand in hand with creating a culture of good *internal* service.

An overarching point behind each of these practices is that both good and bad companies often take steps to measure aspects of the customer experience. Customer Champions, however, go a step further and see their mission as understanding the world of their customers. Some even go so far as to research and explore the lifestyles of their customers, doing the same things these customers do, to understand the direction of their own products and services better. Above all, nearly every best-of-breed company has mechanisms in place to continually see its operations as customers see them. By developing this as a value as well as a process, service becomes a matter of knowledge and intimacy, instead of just policy.

GETTING YOUR POLICIES AND YOUR SERVICE CULTURE IN HARMONY

We tend to dismiss bad customer-service experiences as being the domain of rude people, bad managers, and indifferent businesses. In reality, most organizations create a culture that makes good service either predictable or next to impossible—and they do so by making decisions that take place long before the customer transaction itself. It is here that the values that drive a good or bad service culture are formed. As one example, let's take a look at a recent situation from my own experience with one retail chain, and examine some of the cultural factors behind it.

A TALE OF A BROKEN LAWN MOWER

My wife purchased a new lawn mower from a major chain and barely a week went by before a cheap plastic door on it snapped off as she was mowing between two bushes. Returning this mower to the store's service department for what we thought would be a simple warranty repair, we were instead told that (1) it wasn't covered under warranty, because we couldn't "prove" that we didn't brutally yank the part off ourselves, and (2) even if we did want to have a technician look at it, it would be a very long wait for service.

After silently thanking the service representative for being so helpful, I went out on the sales floor and asked to see the department manager, to plead our case for a repair. In the discussion that followed, I was told:

- A repair was impossible, because service was a different department than sales, and the repair would have to be charged to the service department. However, I *could* return the mower for a full refund, because that was covered under a separate store policy.

- Problems with mowers are tracked on the store's computer systems, and if it were a shoddy part, the chain would stop selling the mower, so therefore it couldn't possibly be a shoddy part!
- We could exchange it for a similar mower. However, that particular mower was on backorder, and the manager had no idea when more would arrive—even though it was going on sale nationally two days later. And no, we could not buy the display model.

In the end, we did return the mower for a refund. A week later, our very same mower appeared again on their sales floor, completely repaired and for sale used at a $70 discount. I purchased it for a second time, essentially getting paid handsomely by the store to have it fix my problem anyway.

Technically, this store satisfied my problem. I not only received a full refund (and a rebate), but also pocketed a substantial amount of money and had the mower fixed besides. Moreover, the transaction was civil and polite on both sides. But this experience left me fascinated by so many aspects of what had happened, such as:

- Why a store would rather take back a used mower, that it would have to fix anyway and resell at a steep discount, rather than simply do the right thing and fix the part.
- Why a department manager had no ability to intercede with the service department of the same store.
- Why it had no idea when a similar mower would arrive, despite the fact that the chain was putting it on sale nationally in a couple of days.
- Why I was given a full refund *and* received a mail-in rebate (and told the store about it), because the people behind the sales counter had no idea how to deal with the rebate.

As luck would have it, one of my colleagues had previously been a senior manager at this store and I couldn't resist discussing this with him to see what he thought of my experience. What he told me provided a fascinating insight about what kind of cultural issues led to this experience with the mower.

Apparently, during his tenure, this chain experienced serious competitive problems from newer discount chains, underwent a management shake-up, and, as a result, decentralized much of the decision-making process that had once come from headquarters. In some ways, this newfound "empowerment" was a good thing. It meant, for example, that stores in Florida could now stock more patio furniture, while stores in the Northeast could order more snowblowers. But it also led to some policies that bordered on the ludicrous. For example:

- This chain has two local stores that are 20 miles apart. One store pays higher wages, and many people who live in the backyard of the other store work for the one further away. But because one store belongs to one regional district and the other to another one, the second store can't raise its wages to match those of the first one, because these wage ranges are set at the district level. So many of the better-quality employees in the area work for the higher-paying store, turnover is very high at the other store, and the chain in effect becomes its own worst competitor.
- Commissioned salespeople in "need" areas (like appliances) would often coast on their jobs, playing cards and passively taking orders, while salespeople in "want" areas (like electronics) would sell aggressively to make their commissions. At the same time, personnel in other areas such as service were strictly paid by the hour and often were in no particular hurry to be helpful. So customers would often see a very different view of the same store, depending on what they were purchasing.

At the same time, many corporate policies from headquarters still remained in place and these had side effects as well:

- The store had generous return policies that were set nationally. But one of its stores in a college town often stood alone in being taken advantage of by crafty students. Many would do things like purchase an expensive computer system, use it for a full school term, and then return it for a refund. Another time, a local fraternity once bought a big-screen TV for Super Bowl weekend and returned it immediately afterwards. By being unable to charge restocking fees or set limits on electronics returns, like their local competitors, my colleague's store was "the largest free rental provider in the area."

- Departments were responsible for their own profit and loss, leading to situations like we experienced with our lawn mower. Providing a small repair was "bad" because it came out of the department's balance sheet, but taking a much larger loss to have me return the merchandise was "good" because it didn't affect the departmental bottom line.

- This store's service department worked on a time-and-materials basis, with little flexibility and strict quotas. In one case, where a customer had purchased $1,500 of appliances from this store, including installation services, the installer found that a standard dryer vent didn't fit the customer's house. Because taking care of this "wasn't policy," the customer had to run out to a hardware store, get the right part, and finish the installation himself, with no help from the store.

So let's bring this full circle to the service experience that my wife and I had. What may seem at first to be a simple matter of shoddy products and indifferent people is, in reality, the end product of certain core values that seemingly run counter to the interests of the company as a whole. The end result of all this is often a Kafkaesque world where policy flies in the face of things such as customer satisfaction, employee retention, profitability, and other good things. As my colleague, who still remains a big fan of this store, puts it: "I am always asking myself how I would do things if it were my name over the storefront. And I get frustrated by these policies."

The same principles that drive this retail chain apply to your business as well. It is very easy to create policies that appear on the surface to make business sense, and then lose track of how these policies ultimately lead to service failures, lost business, and employee turnover. This is why service is not just an isolated initiative unto itself, but rather a by-product of what values stand behind your daily business decisions. Most people look at bad service experiences, such as the one outlined previously, as a failure of the individual. When you dig a little deeper and start seeing these experiences as the failure of a system, you gain a level of competitive insight that few of your competitors will ever have—and take an important step on the road towards developing your own service culture.

SERVICE AS A CORE VALUE

Above all, there is an element to service that can never be captured in a policy manual. When a flight attendant takes an elderly stranded passenger home with her for the night, a hotel employee dashes to the airport with the luggage a guest left behind, or a delivery driver braves flooded roads in a hurricane to deliver vital medical supplies, these people are behaving according to an underlying system of ethics and values. While business processes are important, these ethics and values themselves are, in fact, what drive the success of these business processes.

Service is uniquely a result of other factors, and this remains one of its greatest secrets. You cannot simply exhort people to create excellent service, and then sit back and expect it to occur. Instead, you must tend to the core values behind your organization, and then great service happens. In this sense, service is perhaps more like raising children than producing a product. We cannot work directly at having good children, but by investing love, guidance, education, and respect at all the many little decision points in their lives, these good children eventually emerge.

This family analogy is an appropriate one, because most good families are based around strong family values. In much the same way, organizations with strong service cultures are based around strong organizational values. Customer Champions who develop and nurture these values effectively bridge the gap between customer satisfaction and customer loyalty; their customers won't look for a better deal next time, because they have gone from being simple consumers to becoming part of your family. And like a good family, these relationships ultimately form the basis for a lasting and profitable bond between you and your customers.

Dell Computer

How a Direct-Sales Channel Became a Culture

Few businesses are riskier than being one of the pioneers of a hot new technology, particularly when it changes so rapidly that your products can become obsolete overnight. The personal computer industry was a perfect example: of the top 25 personal computer manufacturers that existed in the early 1980s, nearly 70 percent are out of business today. One, however, became one of the greatest corporate success stories of all time.

Many people nowadays are familiar with the college-boy-makes-good story of CEO Michael Dell, who started selling computers from his dorm room at age 18. Three years later Dell was taking his company public with $30 million in financing, 10 years later it was a $2-billion-a-year operation, and less than 20 years later it became the world's largest computer manufacturer with revenues of more than $30 billion per year. But fewer of these people are aware of the values that created Dell's success; they just know that they are buying reliable computers at competitive prices, from a firm that stays ahead of the technology curve and provides impeccable service.

What is all the more amazing about Dell's success is that it springs from a simple game plan that began in his dorm room days and remains the cornerstone of the company to this day: selling directly to the customer.

In the early 1980s, PC users generally had two alternatives: purchasing an expensive name-brand system from IBM or buying a cheaper "clone" computer that often had shoddier parts and poor service. Dell's objective was to create IBM-compatible computers that offered better performance, better components, and better service than their competition at Big Blue. The key to doing this profitably was to cut out the middleman. Most computers at the time were sold and supported by independent retailers, and Dell's approach took the retail markup out of the pricing equation, helping him sell better systems competitively.

This direct-to-the-consumer sales model was more than just a cost advantage, however; it became a corporate mantra whose ripple effects soon went far beyond competitive pricing, and eventually defined Dell's overall culture. It was a single philosophy that, in turn, led to three of its core business strategies:

1. *Service.* Early computer retailers often were notorious for providing poor service. They generally lacked expertise in the product and had little financial incentive to devote time or resources to customer support. With no middleman, Dell invested heavily in a good service infrastructure. It provided world-class telephone support, led the trend towards providing on-site service, and even today is on the leading edge of "e-support" technologies for managing customer issues online. This, in turn, built a higher comfort level among customers about purchasing systems by telephone or online.

    Perhaps more important, it helped build inroads among corporate users, for whom minimizing downtime was critical. Purchasing "direct from Dell" meant faster turnaround and better service compared with firms with a loose network of so-called authorized repair facilities, and raising the service bar for the whole computer industry soon helped Dell become a staple among the Fortune 500 and others.

2. *Putting demand ahead of supply.* One of Dell's guiding principles today is "a disdain for inventory." As a dorm room operation, Dell essentially had to get orders for computers before building them. Today, it still does exactly the same thing, which drives a streamlined, just-in-time global manufacturing operation. Unlike most manufacturers, it defines inventory in terms of days or even hours instead of weeks. This allows Dell to ship only what has been ordered, and is the linchpin of a collaborative long-term relationship with a few key suppliers, some of whose products, like monitors, never even appear in a Dell factory on its way to the customers.

3. *Customer intimacy.* Dell knows what its customers want better than most technology firms, because its operations are almost totally driven by inbound orders. This gives Dell a strategic head start in knowing what new technologies customers will want and ramping this new technology into the market quicker. In a business where losing the technology lead can be a death sentence, Dell's constant real-time pulse on its customers is a strategic advantage over ven-

dors who make systems, push them into retail channels, and then hope people will buy them.

Dell himself is an unusually hands-on CEO, spending 40 percent of his time with customers, and often during his evenings cruising Internet chat rooms and Web sites for comments about his products. And as an organization, Dell Computer continually seeks ways to leverage its own manufacturing "velocity" for the benefit of customers: for example, major clients can have their own software configurations preloaded as part of the system assembly process, saving clients hours of setup time.

This goal to be direct to the customer eventually led to one of Dell's biggest and most successful gambles—the move to selling and servicing its products via the Internet. A strategy that required both massive investments in infrastructure, as well as training an entire culture to be Net-literate at once, succeeded in a big way. More important, its own sales force had to learn to view the Internet as a sales channel that complemented rather than competed with its own efforts. This move was crucial to Dell's survival, in a world that quickly came to view "direct sales" as going to a Web browser instead of to a telephone. Today more than half of Dell's sales take place online, at costs that could never be duplicated in a bricks-and-mortar environment.

Interestingly, a few stumbles in Dell's early years came when it moved away from its direct sales model, such as overinvesting in inventory, developing new products based on technology instead of customer input, and even a brief foray into selling through the retail market. Today, however, this core philosophy drives a strong workplace environment of service leadership and individual accountability, which, in turn, has built Dell's market position as a trusted supplier of leading-edge technology. For a company that started in a dorm room less than a generation ago, competing with companies the size of IBM, Dell Computer has become a clear example of the market's response to a strong business concept that defined a culture.

7

The Passionate

Business as a Way of Life

The Passionate view their work as much more than just a job; they see it as a mission and a way of life. They see a higher purpose in what they are accomplishing, and this sense of purpose carries both them and their teams to levels of accomplishment that most people can only imagine. Some of the ingredients of a Passionate workplace are:

We foster job-related outside activities. Look at many successful companies and you will find programs that encourage people to develop their talents outside of work—trainers being funded for activities such as Toastmasters, scientists being sent to conferences to present research papers, and even bus drivers being supported in "road-eo" events that show off their driving skills. An organization that recognizes the initiative of its own people breeds a high level of commitment, inside and outside the workplace.

We are very active in using our professional talents in the community. In many cities in the United States, top restaurants do their best cooking to serve a unique clientele—the homeless. The Taste of the Nation program matches the talents of an area's best chefs with a fundraising event that generates substantial contributions to local hunger relief efforts. In a similar manner, businesses ranging from small shops to major corporations often share their talents outside of work to support their local community while taking pride in what they do best.

We see even the most humble of jobs as professions. How enthusiastic can you be about hauling garbage? One afternoon I was teaching a seminar in a Washington, D.C., hotel when the entire class turned to the window as a gleaming, brand-new garbage truck pulled onto the lawn. It was part of a waste-management firm's seminar on its new technology, and the people attending were positively excited about what they were seeing. A couple of attendees explained to us that this truck was part of a state-of-the-art logistics operation—including wireless technology that would communicate with headquarters about how full the truck was—tied into computer systems that would automate the routes of their fleet in real time. Others offered to give a tour of the cab and show off its features. Their pride was obvious, and these people honestly felt that they were the superstars of the trash-hauling business.

Many firms have successful workplaces, but a fortunate few have cultures that go beyond excellence, professionalism, training, and other traditional ingredients of success. For these firms, people also love what they are doing, and their passion for the workplace creates its own set of values. Here we will take a look at what drives firms that go beyond excellence and create a bond between their employees and the workplace.

LOVE OF WORK AS A CULTURE

For all too few firms, culture is defined by a love of work among the people who work there. It is never simply driven by the profession itself. There are firms in glamorous fields such as arts and entertainment with very dysfunctional cultures, and as we have seen, trash-hauling firms who take great pride in their work. More accurately, love of work is a function of who you are and what values drive you. Expertise, innovation, peer dedication and buy-in to broader business goals are all natural by-products of an environment where people have a passion for what they do.

You could sum up Passionate workplaces where employees love what they are doing in one word: professionalism. There is a continuum between a job and a way of life, and many of the most successful cultures foster workplaces that are at least a little of both. It is a hard concept to quantify, but one that you can easily recognize when you see it. The concierge who is a walking encyclopedia of the best nightspots in his city, the pharmaceutical researcher who is earning a Ph.D. in night school, and the team of grocery workers who function with the crack precision of a racing pit crew are all examples of professionalism in action. It is a phenomenon that cuts across the full spectrum of products, services, and work environments, from the largest corporation to the smallest mom-and-pop business.

TAKING THE FAMILY BUSINESS TO A NEW LEVEL

Opeka Auto Repair is a family-owned auto body and repair shop that is a good example of the impact of professionalism in one's life work. It has grown from a home-based garage business to a massive 10,000-square-foot facility in suburban Pittsburgh. Both the father who founded it and the son who now manages it attended top engineering schools, the latter earning a mechanical engineering degree. Between their technical background and a true love of cars, they have gained a strong word-of-mouth reputation for perfectionism in automotive body work and restoration.

A polite, articulate man with a penchant for both working on race cars and reading popular business books, current owner Dale Opeka has hung around cars ever since his youth, and is as much at ease under the hood as he is running a large business. Outside of the shop, Opeka has served on a national committee of automotive service professionals, was part of the National Employer Leadership Council, a leadership development program for youth exploring their careers, and, looking to the future, is grooming his son to follow in the business.

Professionalism can quickly transcend other business success factors, and, in particular, it can be a key differentiating factor for small businesses. Opeka's facility, for example, is in an out-of-the-way location within a metropolitan area that is full of chain auto repair and body shop facilities. Many of them have more convenient locations and hours than he does. But customers still seek out his shop, because of a word-of-mouth reputation that Opeka's is the best.

The same kind of professionalism can be part of any workplace, with the right people and the right values in place. It is one of those intangibles that cannot be measured quantitatively, but creates very tangible results in areas such as productivity, quality, morale, and profitability. Here are some of the factors that drive it.

Mastery of Your Craft

Most people simply do their jobs, but Passionates make it a point to do theirs very well. The impact of this is obvious on a small scale: for example, when you are planning a wedding, many caterers can go through the motions of creating a cake, but the one who creates the *perfect* cake is the one who gets more word-of-mouth business than it can handle. But many people don't realize that the same is true on a large scale as well. When you scratch the surface of many industry-leading firms, you often find a culture that supports doing something better than anyone else does. Whether it takes the form of an individual fortune or the Fortune 500, the link between mastery and market share is stronger than many people realize.

The Desire to Learn More

We are all learning from the moment we are born, but Passionates make it a point to stay educated in their chosen field. An old joke goes, "What do they call the person who graduated last in medical school? Doctor!" In practice, however, what often separates the best physicians from the rest of the pack is how well they keep up with what's new in their field through continuing education and private study. But learning is not just a privilege reserved for professions such as medicine. From meteorologists to prison guards, you will often find trade journals, conferences, and professional societies available for most occupations. And even the most entry-level of positions can and should have the opportunity for further training and development. The best people in any field gravitate towards these kinds of resources, and the best cultures support and nurture their efforts to do so.

A Hunger to Be the Best

There is a competitive aspect to being Passionate as well as a competence one. The need to improve on what's already been done is an important source of self-satisfaction for both individual contributors and teams in an organization. For example, the efforts of scientists and engineers to push the boundaries of computing power have led not only to successful companies but to an entirely new social paradigm where people's personal and professional lives have become increasingly intertwined with personal computers and the Internet. On a smaller scale, a group of lifelong friends in Poland channeled their opposition to Communism in the 1980s into Poland's first independent newspaper, and from there, built their firm Agora into what is now that country's dominant newspaper and radio network. There is no such thing as a business with no further need of improvement, and workplaces that capitalize on this find that even simply undertaking the quest itself changes their culture for the better.

Like any corporate value, this urge can be taken to extremes. One high-end computer manufacturer, for example, once pitted design teams against each other for its new computers, keeping the best team's design and discarding the other. (This approach led to powerful computers at a cost of disenfranchising an entire engineering team, and as a result, most similar firms do not share this design philosophy today.) In much worse cases, the competitive instinct can lead to malfeasance, ranging from corporate espionage to putting individual interests ahead of the interests of the company. But kept in the right balance, the urge to constantly improve can be a strong motivational factor that focuses a team.

An Enlightened Self-Interest

Motivational speaker Zig Ziglar once said, "You can get anything you want, if you help enough other people get what they want." Cultures who foster a path to great responsibility, pay, and respect find that they breed professionalism in return. Deep down inside, everyone asks the question "What's in it for me?" when they decide what kind of emotional investment they will put into the workplace. And in some cases, the direction that they find in their work becomes a guiding force in the rest of their lives.

Every business has a different set of rewards to offer people who contribute to their success, and these help drive what kinds of people build their culture. Large firms have well-established career paths and training programs. Small firms can offer greater responsibilities and often are more open to providing opportunities to nontraditional candidates. Start-up ventures trade a high level of commitment for financial and growth opportunities. Whatever matrix of possibilities you offer, the ability for your team members to reach their personal goals drives your organization's ability to reach its goals.

History is full of successful businesses that are built on taking a job and making a profession of it, or, put another way, taking something that everyone does and doing it just a little bit better. From Lands' End clothes to Häagen-Dazs ice cream to Krispy Kreme doughnuts, the level of expertise and quality can tip the scales in a very nonlinear fashion, from being in the middle of the pack to dominating the marketplace. And this level of success often is far disproportionate to how much better a company is—the fact that it is even 5 percent ahead of the pack makes it stand out head and shoulders from the rest.

More important, becoming Passionate about your work becomes an important driving force in the culture of your entire team. It is never an external force driven by the business itself. However, it is a power that can be harnessed in any business, from all walks of life. Your level of professionalism is the result of choices made in the workplace each and every day, combined with the passion and enthusiasm of the people who make them.

THE INGREDIENTS OF A PASSIONATE WORKPLACE

Ultimately, being Passionate is an individual virtue. It can be nurtured by the right business culture, but it is measured one person at a time. At the same time, certain corporate virtues are common to cultures that are passionate about what they do. The best of these environments are driven by several key factors, including genuine enthusiasm from the top, a clear sense of purpose, the right team members, continuous improvement, and, above all, high goals. Each of these factors plays a role in building the intangibles that drive your team's level of commitment to the workplace.

Genuine Enthusiasm from the Top

It is not unusual to find Continental Airlines CEO Gordon Bethune at the controls of one of his company's jetliners or under an engine cowling— he is a licensed pilot who is type-rated on the Boeing 757 and 767, as well as a licensed aircraft mechanic. When a neighbor of Compaq CEO Michael Capellas had problems with his Compaq computer, Capellas himself came over to fix it. And Colonel Harlan Sanders began his fast-food empire by barnstorming restaurants with a pressure cooker in his car trunk, showing people how to cook chicken. Whatever business you are in, being Passionate for your daily business starts with the person at the top. Leaders set the tone for their management teams, for their hiring practices, and, ultimately, for the enthusiasm that everyone has on the front lines about their products or services.

A Clear Sense of Purpose

Does your frontline team know your firm's mission statement from memory? Could they explain to people what makes your company different from its competitors? If someone asked them why they wanted to work there, what would they answer? Workplaces in which employees know who they are, and where they are going, are powerful forces compared with the vast majority of "just a job" work environments.

The Right Team Members

Would you pick someone who hates rock music to work at a CD store? Or someone who knows nothing about sports for the sales department of a baseball franchise? On a broader scale, too many work environments choose team members who have credentials on paper but no passion for the larger purpose of their business. Conversely, Passionate workplaces tend to seek a similar level of enthusiasm in their new recruits, who, in turn, help self-perpetuate their values across the entire organization.

Continuous Improvement

Few workplaces today haven't heard the term *continuous process improvement,* and fewer still haven't been part of at least some kind of performance improvement initiative. But in a Passionate workplace, the term has an entirely different meaning. Rather than being measured from above, employees are driven from within. For example, 3M allows its scientists to spend up to 15 percent of their time—nearly one day a week—researching any job-related area that they wish. The results of this investment of time include advances such as 3M's Post-It notes, among other innovations.

High Goals

Nearly every workplace claims that its goal is to be the best. It simply doesn't sound right to state publicly that "our employees have an objective of just getting by every day." But the reality of daily work life is often exactly that. By comparison, Passionate workplaces often set high goals for themselves—specific, reachable high goals. For example, Texas's Andarko Petroleum set its sights on finding oil and natural gas in places where most exploration firms had given up because of challenging geography or environmental conditions. Its success on the cutting edge of oil exploration, combined with savvy business partnerships, boosted its sales by a factor of nearly ten within two years—helping Andarko recently land squarely in the middle of the Fortune 500.

At the same time, you can't just sit in a corner office and dictate these goals. A subtle point that many managers miss is that you need both a goal and a game plan. When people buy in to the game plan, they will pull together to reach the goal. Conversely, as two major corporations discovered in the 1990s, just blindly raising the performance bar can do significant damage.

WHEN SALES GOALS BACKFIRE

It is widely believed that unrealistic sales goals hurt the credibility and market share of two of America's market giants in the early 1990s—**IBM** and **Sears.** In the former case, a dictum that IBM would reach $100 billion per year in revenue by 1990 caused the computer giant to overextend itself, focus on short-term financial results, and, worst of all, ignore its lifelong traditions of long-term sales and service relationships with its customers. Actual revenues barely exceeded half its target, and the fallout in later years included a $23-billion charge against earnings, widespread layoffs, and an eventual change in top management.

In Sears's case, aggressive sales goals and a commission-based compensation structure was blamed for a rash of incidents where customers were charged for unneeded auto repairs over a two-year period. Sears management initially dismissed the allegations as isolated incidents, but following action by state and federal authorities, it eventually scrapped its commission scheme in favor of a system based on customer-satisfaction levels.

Both IBM and Sears recovered from these incidents, the former becoming one of the hot growth stocks of the late 1990s by changing its goals to once again get closer to its customers. And ironically, by trading its financial goals of reaching $100 billion in sales for a more strategic one of reclaiming the services market for business computing, IBM's revenues are now fast approaching its original $100-billion-per-year revenue milestone as of this writing. This new, more customer-focused business strategy has increased annual revenues by nearly 40 percent from its low point in the 1990s.

Each of these traits involves values from the top of an organization, which then become part of the daily operations of the workplace. They represent a strong desire to win expressed as core values, rather than simple exhortations to work harder. In a sense, you can draw a parallel between Passionate workplaces and a successful sports team:

- They are unified in the pursuit of a goal.
- There is constant coaching and improvement.
- Everyone is a contributor.
- They know their roles in an overall game plan.
- They are doing what they love. No one ever "works" a sporting event, but they all "play" it.

At a deeper level, both Passionate work cultures and successful sports teams revolve around dedication, commitment, and a healthy sense of group competitiveness. They both require direction from the top and buy-in from the team on the field. But when these factors come together, the end result is a culture in which people motivate themselves to succeed rather than take orders from management. Thus, while the groundwork for these cultures is often sown from the top, the end results always percolate upwards from the people on the front line.

SUPPORTING THE WORK-LIFE CONTINUUM

Sometimes, one of the best things you can do for your culture is to foster an environment where the things that people do at work go home with them. Whether it is the auto shop employees who race cars off-hours, the cartoonists who paint serious art off-hours, or the news reporters who write books, high-commitment workplaces nurture an environment where work interests become life interests. Then, in turn, people's off-hours passions become a tangible part of your talent pool during the day—sometimes in a very direct way.

WANTED: People to Play Video Games

A cartoon once showed a child in front of a video game, while his parents daydreamed about want ads for high-paying jobs as video game players. For about 200 people who work for **Nintendo's** help line, that is exactly how their careers turned out. People nationwide call this group for help and advice playing Nintendo's games, ranging from young children all the way to one group of elderly players teleconferencing from a retirement home. These "game counselors" also perform quality-assurance testing on games in development, and travel around the country teaching people how to play new games, in addition to manning the company's pay-per-call number for game-playing assistance. Their qualifications include good technical and interpersonal skills, and, oh yes, they are all extremely good video game players.

Other people take what they do well on the job and use it for the good of the community, or for the good of the world. Many people take pride in charitable and pro bono work that helps others, while providing themselves with a chance to show off their greatest strengths. Whether it is doctors or lawyers who staff free clinics, contractors who renovate homes for civic programs, or professionals who volunteer for global relief efforts, good deeds often follow a genuine sense of pride in one's profession. Even very specialized experts often find ways to give back something tangible to the rest of society, such as shown in this example from a California consulting firm.

THE ROCKET SCIENTISTS WHO SAVED A PELICAN

In the 1980s, people in southern California were horrified to read about a pelican that had been deliberately maimed by vandals. The pelican's beak had been sawed off, making it unable to catch food, and dooming it to death by slow starvation. When wildlife experts found this hungry, dehydrated bird, they tried to nurse it back to health, but held out little hope that it could ever be returned to the wild.

After hearing about this story, a local aerospace consulting firm decided to try and do something about it. They obtained measurements of the bird's remaining beak structure, did some computer simulations of the forces that a new beak would need to withstand, and designed and built a new beak from space-age composite materials that could be attached to the bird and allow the bird to function naturally. The pelican was eventually released into the wild, the company received considerable public relations exposure for its efforts, and later it eventually grew to become part of a major quarter-billion-dollar-per-year engineering software and consulting firm.

Still others find ways to show off their expertise to educate or entertain the public. These organizations serve a dual goal of creating something fun, while teaching people about themselves and fostering the growth of their own culture:

- In Huntsville, Alabama, aerospace engineers from regional firms such as Boeing and NASA take on the public in an annual paper airplane contest.
- Every year, motorcycle cops from around the country descend on Coral Springs, Florida, to show off their riding skills in a friendly competition to raise money for charity.
- The civil engineering department at Cornell University once sponsored a regular "concrete canoe" competition for its students, where they would design and race boats constructed from concrete. (And yes, they floated!)

This kind of outside involvement can represent an opportunity to define and promote your own culture. Company-sponsored activities may be opportunistic efforts, such as the heavy-equipment firms who raced men and machinery to lower Manhattan following the September 11, 2001, tragedy, or ongoing efforts such as food donations from a restaurant or grocery chain. They can also be highly personal to specific causes, such as the involvement of many professional sports teams in youth sports. Either way, the rewards go far beyond good publicity; they often add meaning to work life, by supporting the larger meaning of life.

This desire to bring your profession into the rest of your life, and into the community, cannot be forced. But it can be nurtured. How supportive your culture is with individual investments of time, or corporate investments of funds, often determines how likely people are to follow their professional interests outside the workplace. These decision points may include areas such as:

- Allowing people to be involved with professional activities during work time
- Investing time and resources in your local community
- Lending facilities, leadership, or structure to grassroots efforts aligned with your culture
- Donating your business expertise in times of need
- Supporting individual initiatives to use their expertise outside of work

Your level of involvement in outside professional interests must be appropriate and must ultimately cost-justify itself, in particular, to remove the temptation to cut it back when times are leaner. Once this trend becomes established, its benefits can go far beyond what happens in the community, and into the daily productivity and motivation of your normal work life. It becomes a very tangible investment in your future and ultimately a cornerstone of the business personality behind a Passionate culture.

SERVING THE GREATER GOOD

Perhaps the highest expression of a Passionate work culture is when organizations devote themselves in support of something greater than themselves. Whether the goal is putting a man on the moon or eradicating world hunger, a focus on the greater good not only improves our lives, but also celebrates the dignity and importance of those doing the work. Let's examine one organization in detail, and see how its cultural values revolve around a unique view of providing service to others.

SMALL IS BEAUTIFUL: Making a Difference at Concern America

Most American physicians can look forward to high-paying positions and a comfortable lifestyle. But for one doctor who served as a volunteer for **Concern America,** his choice was an unsalaried position working in remote villages of El Salvador. One week might find him going from village to village vaccinating people and treating acute problems, another week might involve training local "health promoters" to work within their villages, while other times would find him meeting with government health officials to try to gain support for further grassroots health efforts.

On the surface, the role of this physician and others like him has been to improve public health in a country that had been racked by civil war and poverty. At a deeper level, however, his mission was to empower local people to understand, manage, and improve their own level of health care, as a partner rather than as an "expert." By the time his tenure in the field was complete, he left behind communities with their own local health care paraprofessionals, gardens of medicinal plants to stock village pharmacies, a legacy of training on public health and nutrition, and, more important, people with an active voice in their own health care system.

Operating with a budget under $1 million per year, less than that of an average automobile dealership, Concern America has made a critical contribution to refugee and relief efforts in Central America, Mexico, Africa, and elsewhere. According to director Marianne Loewe, its size and scale is intentional. "We really feel that small is beautiful. Of course, we want to have enough to cover our expenses, but at our current size, I personally know every person working in the field." At any given time, Concern America has between 20 and 30 people serving for two years or more of international fieldwork.

The popular image of a relief organization is one of experts swooping in to rescue desperate people. Concern America disdains this stereotype and director Marianne Loewe underscores its focus on empowering people to change their own lives as they emerge from difficult circumstances. "We are part of the building of civil society, and in many of these places where we work in the aftermath of civil war, the garments of civil society have been rent. So, we're there to help provide a space where people can start to build trust again. Our people, as outside people, bring a certain dimension of objectivity to the environment. And when we show that we really trust people, it gives them the space to start trusting each other."

Concern America borrows much of its philosophy in the field from Paolo Freire, a Brazilian educator devoted to helping people understand their own reality and then being able to transform it. Rather than seeing teaching as a process of depositing knowledge into people's heads, its approach is to facilitate reality-based learning using words and phrases from people's everyday lives. For example, indigenous farmers may learn to read by learning words from their everyday reality, such as crops and corn. From there, they can start to understand issues such as how prices are low because everyone sells at harvesttime, while costs are high because they must constantly replenish their small supplies. And then, in the long term, they understand that reality can help them make a difference in their own lives by seeking solutions such as using silos or seeking better grain storage facilities.

A situation like this is a good example of how Concern America volunteers help empower people, but more important, it underscores how Concern America's size works to its advantage. The close, grassroots relationship necessary between an organization of its size and the people it serves spares the group the luxury of endless projects and expensive blunders. It also focuses Concern America on high-impact projects where needs are most critical, such as cooking and sanitation improvements in the impoverished Petén region of Guatemala, or a recent initiative to train mental health workers among refugees from war-ravaged Sierra Leone. In efforts like these, Concern America refers to the people it trains as "multipliers," creating self-sustaining projects that touch more and more people as time goes on.

One program that perhaps typifies Concern America's approach to relief work is its Adopt-a-Volunteer program, where contributors sponsor one of their field workers rather than a child being helped. Sponsors receive regular updates from the Concern America volunteers they are supporting, containing very frank, factual discussions of the successes and frustrations of their personal fieldwork in recent months. This program helps its supporters get to know the volunteers and their work, and sends an important symbolic message of respect, equality, and dignity for the people it serves. As a result of both its philosophy and success, Concern America attracts a steady stream of volunteer applicants, and it is not unusual for people in the field to extend their volunteer assignments.

The same values that drive Concern America can be applied to any group with goals that transcend the normal worklife, and it is not limited to nonprofit organizations or to scientists trying to cure cancer. *Any* organization can decide to focus on serving its public, and become the very best at it. There is a key difference in focus between selling products and improving lives, and those leaders who promote the latter breed an entirely different level of commitment among their teams. In a very real sense, the essence of a Passionate workplace is encapsulated within those who seek to make the world a better place.

PUTTING PASSION TO WORK IN YOUR CULTURE

Passion cannot be forced. A "corporate passion" initiative would probably be doomed to failure, and simply putting the word in your mission statement will not make passion happen. But every day, your workplace is faced with decisions that help your team decide whether jobs become professions, and professions become a way of life. It is a goal that cannot be attacked directly, but becomes a by-product of the choices you make when employees ask you for continuing education, ongoing professional development, or support of projects outside the workplace. It also reflects the level of commitment that your top people, and the people who manage your front lines, have for what they are doing.

Perhaps most important, a Passionate workplace is not something that you can write a check for. Businesses may spend a million dollars on automation, or a billion dollars on facilities, and still be in worse shape than when they started. But kindling the enthusiasm of your team generally requires little in the way of costs or infrastructure. It does start with values, which fuel the decision-making process behind issues affecting people on your team. And these values can ultimately lead you far beyond the point where most business processes leave off.

We all have an innate need to be worthwhile and important. By nurturing this natural impulse in your workplace, and harnessing the energy it produces, you can create an environment that transcends normal logic about motivation, work ethic, and productivity. Once again, it all starts with well-intentioned business decisions and the values behind them. By supporting an authentic passion for the work that drives your organization, much of what drives your success will follow naturally from there.

The Creative Spirit
Putting the Art First at Cirque du Soleil

Audacity is a word that is rarely applied to a successful business, but at Cirque du Soleil, it is a defining virtue, and, in fact, was once the only character trait mentioned in its mission statement. Audacity fueled the beginnings of Cirque du Soleil, when a group of Quebec street performers risked everything they had in the 1980s to form a touring company built around breathtaking human performances. Today, the same audacity drives an enterprise that now surpasses a quarter of a billion dollars in annual revenue, yet still retains the same go-for-broke spirit of stretching the limits of human creativity and performance.

For the uninitiated, Cirque du Soleil (literally, "circus of the sun") is a cultural phenomenon that far transcends the common circus. Its productions are awe-inspiring and ethereal, combining acrobats, clowns, music, and dance within a common artistic theme. Japanese drummers descend from the ceiling seemingly suspended in midair, teams of acrobats execute with precision in routines that stretch the limits of belief, and hip, streetwise clowns make the audience erupt with laughter. And this undercurrent of audacity flows underneath all of it—no human emotions are taboo, no convention within the bounds of family entertainment can't be challenged, no limit of human performance can't be stretched. The results are productions that careen wildly back and forth between wistfulness, laughter, and amazement, designed to fulfill its stated mission to "invoke the imagination, provoke the senses, and evoke the emotions of people around the world."

Since Cirque du Soleil's humble beginnings in the 1980s, this sense of audacity has struck a major chord with its audiences—its productions have delighted more than 30 million people in the decade and a half of its existence. Its appearances sell out more than 97 percent of its available seats, with a fan base that includes many major public figures and entertainers. Recent productions range from *Quidam*, an acrobatic fantasy built around a world-weary young girl transported from home, to the ambitious O^{TM} (from the French word for water, *eau*), staged around a permanent 1.5-million-gallon aquatic stage in Las Vegas's Bellagio hotel. Today, it is a worldwide entertainment empire, with eight simultaneous touring shows as well as permanent engagements in Las Vegas and Walt Disney World, and is home to more than 2,400 performers, musicians, technicians, and support staff.

At a personal level, this sense of audacity attracts a worldwide troupe of performing artists who are challenged to constantly exceed themselves. They draw strength from the amazed reaction of their audiences—in the words of trampolinist Krystian Sawicki, a menacing strongman in Cirque du Soleil's *La Nouba*, "Children love my character! This makes my work more enjoyable. They call me 'strongman,' 'evil man,' or 'monster,' and try to imitate me." A performing role in Cirque du Soleil represents a dream come true for its artists, many of whom train for years in preparation for their roles. And they work in perhaps the world's only major corporation whose senior management were once stilt-walkers and fire-eaters—a key factor in how one of Canada's major entertainment industries still focuses on the interests of the performer.

This sense of audacity-as-a-virtue is perhaps at its peak in the creation of new shows, which balance a collaborative team effort with an imperative to ignore past triumphs, and start everything anew from scratch. Longtime composer Rene Dupere described the process in an interview for the Melbourne (Australia) *Sunday Herald Sun:* "We are French so we discuss many things—philosophy, life, love, death—until we come to an issue we want in the show." Then, once a core concept is established, different team members develop their views of this concept as it would apply to areas such as costuming, music, acrobatics, or dance. Between then and a finished production lies a great deal of interaction and negotiation between teams, as the new show gradually takes shape.

While experiencing major growth as a corporation, Cirque du Soleil is still unquestionably a creative enterprise. At its sprawling, $40-million headquarters in Montreal, it is possible to look out an office window and see gymnasts or acrobats performing—or for anyone to take a virtual tour via Cirque du Soleil's Internet site. Its headquarters building is designed around massive open indoor spaces, with a focus on workspace for the performers. A family atmosphere prevails at both headquarters and on location, and above all, the one core rule is that people work collaboratively. Star treatment is shunned, and even top performers are expected to pitch in with the everyday operations of the show.

Within the company are dual career tracks for creative and management professionals, and one need not transition from one side to the other to advance within Cirque du Soleil. Employees share 10 percent of the company's profits, with another 1 percent invested in working with at-risk youth. And this latter investment is much more than just blank check–writing: its Cirque du Monde program uses circus arts programs on every continent to teach youth living on the fringe to "draw on their marginal status in forging a new type of relationship with a society that has often rejected them." This program, administered in cooperation with youth agencies worldwide, openly shares a bond with the founders' own early days as street-performers among a then indifferent public.

Perhaps the most important symbol of Cirque du Soleil's commitment to its performers is its decision to remain a privately held company. Its size, growth, and profitability make an attractive target for outside investors, whose capital would greatly enrich the financial position of the company's stakeholders, but the company prefers its independence. As current president Gay Laliberté told *Maclean's* magazine, "One year, we might decide not to make a profit, in order to develop a new show. Or if we decide to delay a development, we don't want shareholders asking us why we didn't do what we promised." He speaks with the voice of someone who hasn't forgotten the days when Cirque du Soleil's early productions were daring, make-or-break artistic decisions on which the future of the company hinged.

Today, its independence allows the circus the artistic freedom to experiment with both new productions and new markets for the future. It can keep the same focus on the art itself that guided its leaders when they were young, hip performers who created a circus in the streets. In an open letter on Cirque du Soleil's Web site, Laliberté states, "A group of young entertainers got together to amuse audiences, see the world, and have fun doing it. Every year the audiences get bigger, we continue to discover new places and ideas, and we're still having fun." As a result of this philosophy—and never letting go of the audacity that drove it many years ago—Cirque du Soleil continues to build a bright future by letting its creative spirit guide its business interests.

8

The Visionaries
Leadership That Seeks a Higher Purpose

Visionaries are the most important people in any business culture—and often the most highly rewarded, as leadership and vision go hand in hand. Visionaries are people who set the direction for where a business is going, establish the path to get there, and define goals that inspire an entire organization. Here are some of the traits they share in common:

We develop most leaders from within. In many of the most successful firms, leadership isn't something that is parachuted in from outside; it grows and develops from within people who understand and buy in to the culture. In organizations ranging from Southwest Airlines, whose current CEO served as her predecessor's secretary over a quarter century ago, to UPS, where a high percentage of its executive management started out driving trucks for the company, leadership is often synonymous with living and breathing the firm's values.

Our employees are focused on the "big picture" of our organization. Try this experiment sometime: ask your frontline employees what your company's gross revenues were the past year. Or what its business strategy is for the future. If you get blank stares in response, you are in the majority, and that represents a competitive advantage for leading cultures, who almost universally keep employees knowledgeable and focused on the company's mission.

Our upper management communicates with all employees at least weekly. Look at firms who are well known for their cultures nowadays—FedEx, Hewlett-Packard, Continental Airlines, and others—and you will find that a surprising number of them provide weekly or even daily updates to employees from the company's management.

In the United States, an ideal example of a Visionary is our nation's president. Formal job qualifications for the position are almost nonexistent. With few prerequisites other than being a natural-born U.S. citizen over 35 years of age, nearly anyone can be elected to a position that commands the armed forces, conducts foreign policy, appoints judges, and has veto power over the laws that run the country. In recent history, we have had former actors, lawyers, and even peanut farmers elected to serve at the helm of the greatest democracy in the world.

So why are there fewer requirements to become president than to become a high school principal? Because what we are really electing is a Visionary. Someone who will tell us that we will put a man on the moon within ten years, lead us out of a recession, or create determination and hope when we fall under a terrorist attack. Someone who will inspire us to become part of something greater than ourselves. And no job qualifications, work experience, or graduate degrees confer the ability to possess that kind of vision.

At the same time, a high school principal needs to be a Visionary as well. So does a factory foreman, an accounting supervisor, or the CEO of your business. Vision from the top is just as important in your workplace as it is in the leadership of a nation, because it provides the direction from which every other decision flows. Your culture is ultimately determined either by values or by human nature, and the vision you create from the top of any organization—of any size—is what filters down your values to each of your daily business decisions.

In a recent speech at Cornell University, American Express chairman and CEO Kenneth Chenault stated that "the purpose of a CEO is to define reality and give hope, leading by values and beliefs." The same is true for leaders at any level—defining these core values and beliefs and then providing the vision for where these values will lead is central to success or failure in any size workplace. In a sense, a leader's mission represents the ultimate sales responsibility: selling your own team on its mission and then seeing this mission come to fruition. This responsibility comes with a commensurate reward—the opportunity to develop a business culture in the image of your own beliefs and watch it drive the success of an entire team.

ONE KEY VALUE

Leadership is inherently nonlinear. You don't succeed at it based on how many hours you put in, how much paperwork you do, or how many rules you create. You are judged purely and simply on results. This means that as a Visionary, the power of your ideas becomes much more important than just the magnitude of your efforts. And sometimes, true leadership is as simple as establishing the one key value that defines who you are. In the case of Fox News Channel, its one key value of fair and balanced reporting has helped catapult it over larger competitors to become the most-watched cable news channel.

FOX NEWS CHANNEL— IMPARTIALITY IS OUR MANTRA

When the Fox News Channel first went on the air in 1996, few people saw the need for yet another 24-hour news channel to compete with the likes of existing networks such as CNN and MSNBC. But today, it has become the David and Goliath story of the broadcast industry. Still less than a third the size of its largest competitor CNN, it now commands similar ratings and often beats CNN in prime time.

John Moody, Fox's senior vice president for news editorial, sums up its success in one word: impartiality. "It is our mantra. It is the integument of our product. It is as inextricably a part of us as belief in eventual salvation is to the Catholic Church—if you don't believe in it, why be here? We will not succeed if we don't hew closely to the notion of impartiality, and fair and balanced news."

This sense of impartiality obviously plays a key role in Fox's programming. For example, its highly rated evening talk show *Hannity and Colmes* is co-hosted by two respected commentators from opposite ends of the political spectrum, and its news analysts run the gamut from Republican Contract with America architect Newt Gingrich to Clinton-era Mideast envoy Dennis Ross. But it has an even stronger presence behind the scenes. According to Moody, "It is imprinted on everything we do, from editorial meetings, to story selection, to what anchors and reporters say on the air, to teasers for upcoming segments. It is simply a part of our being." And viewers, in turn, have picked up on this, flocking in droves to what was once a small upstart that Moody himself still describes as "scrappy" and "unexpectedly successful."

Perhaps it is this sense of impartiality that drives an internal culture with news reporting at its core. Fox News chief Roger Ailes is a veteran political insider, and Moody is a former international bureau chief and correspondent who still views himself as "a journalist in a suit." So, for example, when correspondents set up shop in war-torn regions around the world, they hear from the top brass every single day. According to Moody, "I have never forgotten the advice that I got from one of my own vice presidents when I was a bureau chief: 'Always trust your people in the field.' As soon as you start acting like all wisdom resides at command central, you are not going to get ground-level information, and you'll lose sight of the story." Because of this trust, many people at Fox simply work harder—during the September 11, 2001, tragedy, for example, some staffers didn't go home for more than three days to keep their coverage rolling.

For Fox News, the idea of impartiality has created a clarity of mission that puts its goal of eventually becoming the world's top news network within reach. For Southwest Airlines, the idea of turning around an aircraft twice as fast as anyone else has created a cult-like level of teamwork that allows low-fare airline service to be consistently profitable. And for Ritz-Carlton hotels, the idea of treating employees as equals to the guests they serve has created the unparalleled levels of service that drive a premium-price hotel chain. All these businesses have substantial competition. None of them pioneered their respective products or services. And none of them became leaders just because their policies, procedures, or credit ratings were different. They all succeeded because of one key value.

This means that your success is tied in, more than anything else, with *your* key value. It doesn't depend on your price point: Southwest is the lowest-priced product in its market and Ritz-Carlton is one of the highest. It doesn't depend on your past reputation: most baby boomers remember when Made in Japan meant cheap, inferior products until their key value—high manufacturing quality—took hold. Even a strong balance sheet doesn't always guarantee success: ValuJet had a solid cash position at the time of its 1996 grounding, and, in fact, acquired another airline in the process of later changing its corporate identity. For most businesses, long-term success revolves around forming that one key value, and putting it into play. And being a Visionary is what ultimately makes it happen.

So what is your organization's key value? If you asked a random group of employees what your core value is, would they all give you the same answer? If not, you would join the vast majority of businesses in the world today. Whether you are a frontline workplace supervisor or the CEO of a multinational corporation, you have an opportunity to change the whole nature of your organization by putting forth that one central idea that is larger than all of you—one that captivates your team and becomes a mission for everyone involved. When it comes to a business culture, a leader may have to face many challenging tactical issues, but the essence of being a Visionary is to find the one key value that, in turn, drives your ultimate level of success.

SELLING THE VISION

Once you have defined your vision—your one key value—that idea must resonate within your team and become part of its internal belief system. Here is where successful leaders ultimately make their mark: average ones set goals and exhort people to reach them, while strong ones create a vision that becomes its own motivation. While most leaders set financial or business milestones for their organizations, the Visionary who can also create a sense of corporate identity is often the key factor behind an enduring business culture.

A good example is Johnson & Johnson's famous Credo. Long before mission statements and vision statements became fashionable, company chief Robert Wood Johnson created a detailed statement of values for his company. When penned in 1943, it helped propel what was then a family medical supplies business to global leadership, and served as an important precursor to what we now call corporate culture. This classic corporate affirmation reads as follows:

OUR CREDO

We believe our first responsibility is to the doctors, nurses, patients, to mothers and fathers, and all others who use our products and services. In meeting their needs, everything we do must be of high quality. We must constantly strive to reduce our costs in order to maintain reasonable prices. Customers' orders must be serviced promptly and accurately. Our suppliers and distributors must have an opportunity to make a fair profit.

We are responsible to our employees, the men and women who work with us throughout the world. Everyone must be considered as an individual. We must respect their dignity and recognize their merit. They must have a sense of security in their jobs. Compensation must be fair and adequate, and working conditions clear, orderly, and safe. We must be mindful of ways to help our employees fulfill their family responsibilities. Employees must feel free to make suggestions and complaints. There must be equal opportunity for employment, development, and advancement for those qualified. We must provide competent management, and their actions must be just and ethical.

We are responsible to the communities in which we live and work, and to the world community as well. We must be good citizens—support good works and charities and bear our fair share of taxes. We must encourage civic improvements and better health and education. We must maintain in good order the property we are privileged to use, protecting the environmental and natural resources.

Our final responsibility is to our stockholders. Business must make a sound profit. We must experiment with new ideas. Research must be carried on, innovative programs developed, and mistakes paid for. New equipment must be purchased, new facilities provided, and new products launched. Reserves must be created to provide for adverse times. When we operate according to these principles, the stockholders should realize a fair return.

This one-page document proposed the then radical notion that customers and employees rank ahead of the interests of shareholders—and that if you treat them well, all parties will ultimately profit. The concepts behind this credo helped transform Johnson & Johnson from a family medical supplies business to its current position as a $20-billion-per-year global leader in the health care marketplace.

The principles behind this Credo were most visibly put to the test in the 1980s, when the Tylenol tragedy served as a defining moment in Johnson & Johnson's culture. After several people died from taking tampered Tylenol capsules laced with cyanide, the company's management launched an active and aboveboard response to the problem. It quickly removed its products from the shelves, senior management made themselves freely available to discuss the incident in press conferences and media appearances, and the product itself was quickly redesigned to address the public's concerns with product tampering. As a result, the Tylenol brand suffered no long-term damage in the marketplace. More important, the incident cast a great deal of light on Johnson & Johnson's corporate citizenship, and its stock in the public consciousness rose substantially after the incident.

Today, employees still take part in a regular survey and assessment process to make sure that Johnson & Johnson continues to do business according to the guidelines set down in the Credo, and that these values remain an organization-wide commitment. For example, a colleague of mine worked for a firm that was eventually acquired by Johnson & Johnson and was pleasantly surprised at how quickly its workplace culture changed to reflect the Credo's ideals. As a result, the same principles that were set down in the 1940s, and that guided the company's reaction to the Tylenol tampering crisis generations later, continue to drive the company's operations today.

Perhaps the single biggest mistake that many leaders make is presuming that simply declaring a vision or a goal will make it so. Many people from the baby-boom generation remember President Gerald Ford's famous "WIN button" speech in 1974, when he urged everyone to make personal sacrifices to help tame high inflation and wore a red button with an acronym for Whip Inflation Now. Rather than inspiring people, the WIN button became the butt of late-night talk-show jokes and a campy piece of memorabilia, while inflation remained at double-digit levels well into the next year. Here are some key factors why Visionaries do succeed in selling their message:

Personal Commitment

New York Yankees owner George Steinbrenner is famous (and at times infamous) for his personal involvement in building the Yankees dynasty of the late 20th century—and yet love him or hate him, many of baseball's top stars consistently want to be Yankees. Wendy's late founder Dave Thomas's favorite meal was reportedly a Wendy's Single hamburger, french fries, chili, a Frosty, and a diet Coke, and the sincerity he brought to his television commercials raised the company's consumer brand identity near to that of competitors who outspent Wendy's four-to-one in advertising. In cases like these, a leader's personal passion and commitment is often a catalyst for others to share his or her enthusiasm and spread the company's mission among everyone on the team.

What's In It for Them

One of the surest ways to help people champion the organization's interests is to marry these goals with the employees' personal interests. Firms who make it a point to look out for their employees' success frequently drive their own success as well, as evidenced by the recent growth of home improvement chain Lowe's.

LOWE'S—SHARING FINANCIAL REWARDS WITH ITS ASSOCIATES

Employees of home improvement giant Lowe's may earn retail-level wages, but many of them can retire with substantial nest eggs through employee stock and matching savings plans. The retailer contributes nearly 5 percent of each full-time employee's salary in Lowe's stock, and this percentage can more than double based on corporate growth. The chain openly touts the ability to retire rich as part of its recruiting publicity, and as a result, its 100,000-strong employee base is keenly aware of their personal impact on the company's performance and share price. Already the 14th-largest retailer in the United States, the company's success has led to a growth spurt where new stores are being constructed at the rate of more than two per week.

Financial rewards are, of course, far from the only way to capture the motivation of your employees. Firms that invest heavily in education and training, promote from within, or foster individual professional growth also harness employee self-interest to everyone's benefit. But there must be a commensurate reward, whether psychic, tangible, or both, for the level of commitment that you expect towards the organization's goals.

Understanding the Big Picture

Intrinsic motivation is driven by every individual understanding his or her importance to the big picture, which means treating employees as owners when it comes to sharing information. This concept has been taken to extremes—like one 1980s technology firm that once openly posted everyone's salaries—but every firm can define the right kind of information flow to make its team part of the overall process.

SPRINGFIELD REMANUFACTURING AND "OPEN BOOK" MANAGEMENT

Several years ago, Springfield Remanufacturing CEO Jack Stack became well known for his book *The Great Game of Business,* which proposed an "open book" management style where every person on the team had detailed visibility about their firm's financial performance—and their contributions to this bottom line. Springfield's own story represented a dramatic turnaround: following its 1983 divestiture by foundering parent company International Harvester, its employee ownership began as a desperate measure by Stack and his colleagues to save their own 119 jobs. Within a decade they grew nearly fivefold, employees remained highly literate about the firm's balance sheet, and the open book concept has now spread to dozens of other major firms worldwide.

Beyond each of these factors, perhaps the most important role of a Visionary is to convey the higher purpose of an organization's efforts. Here is one useful way to look at this mission: if you asked your employees why they worked for you, what would they say? Would they proudly say, "I'm making a difference in one of the best organizations in the world" or would it sound more like, "This is just a job."? The knowledge that people are saving lives, improving other businesses, or even just creating a good public example are strong factors in team buy-in towards an organization's goals.

Too many companies convey the following unspoken but very real mission to their employees: "Let's make lots of money for our stockholders." As a result, people often feel like little more than costs to be reduced, motivation and service quality never get out of the starting gate, and doing the minimum amount of work required to pick up a paycheck becomes an end unto itself. This can feed a lack of respect and trust towards employees that eventually becomes a self-fulfilling prophecy, as organizations fail under the weight of their own poor performance. Conversely, in the best workplaces, Visionaries foster a sense of mission that creates its own enthusiasm and performance.

DEVELOPING THE LEADERS WHO CARRY THE VISION

One spring day in 2001, a gathering of educational and business leaders in New York State came together to discuss a looming problem—more than 60 percent of the people in leadership positions in its schools would be retiring in the next three to five years. Already hard-pressed school districts were turning to nontraditional candidates, retired superintendents, and other alternatives to cope with a growing staffing crisis.

After a few opening remarks, state Education Commissioner Richard Mills stepped to the podium and addressed the issue head-on. "We don't have a leadership shortage at all. We have more leaders than we will ever need, right here and now. They are people teaching in our schools who think that they will be teaching for a long time. Someone needs to go to them and say, 'You need to think about being a principal.' There are people who are principals who think that they will be principals for a long time. Someone needs to go to them and say, 'You need to think about being a superintendent.' We need to tell them that they are being called to leadership, and that they need to answer that call."

The situation that Dr. Mills is referring to is a global one. Too many people spend every day of their working lives doing their jobs as assembly line workers, computer programmers, or whatever, and are never given responsibilities that challenge them as leaders—tasks that involve working with teams, strategic responsibility, or profit and loss. Then, when opportunities arise for people to take on more leadership, no one is ready to step up to the plate—and leaders, who may or may not fit the culture, are then recruited from the outside.

If there is one trait common to Visionaries in companies of any size, it is an investment in developing leadership from within. The Boatyard Grill, for example, grooms many of its 100 restaurant employees for future management roles by giving them "test flights" as shift leaders, trainers, or closing crew members. Software vendor The CBORD Group has developed a formal management succession planning effort among its 250-person staff, including management training on developing team members, and team workshops on leadership skills. And on a much larger scale, General Electric's legendary CEO Jack Welch spent nearly a decade grooming a core of possible successors within GE, before choosing Jeffrey Immelt to succeed him in 2001. As Dr. Mills told his fellow educators, companies must call people well before the need, and coach and nurture them as future leaders.

This need to preserve your culture through leadership cuts through every stage of the organization, particularly its early years. The classic business-school conundrum of a growth company is how early leaders often lack the skills needed to take it to the next level. Apple Computer's transfer of power from technopreneur Steve Jobs to former Pepsi Chairman John Scully is one textbook example of how a company was turned over to professional management, sacked its founding leaders, and changed. Eventually, Apple lost its leadership position in the growing personal computer market, and more important its vision for who it was and what it stood for. It became a niche-market player in such areas as desktop publishing, printing, and multimedia, while the booming personal computer market roared past it in the late 1980s and early 1990s.

By comparison, leading cultures tend to have remarkable stability of leadership. In his book *Discovering the Soul of Service,* Texas A&M professor Leonard Berry examined the executive ranks of 14 leading service cultures, and found CEO tenures that generally measured in decades. Many long-standing corporate giants still retain their original top executives, including FedEx's Fred Smith, Chick-fil-A's Truett Cathy, and The Container Store's co-founders Kip Tindell and Garrett Boone. And ironically, even Apple Computer, currently enjoying a resurgence in popularity within the Internet generation with its plug-and-play iMac systems, is once again led by its old chairman Steve Jobs.

Developing your own leaders is an important part of growth, but at the same time, not all businesses feel they can develop their top leadership from within. And sometimes they are correct. Whether you are a work group that feels it needs someone with good supervisory skills, a small service business that needs a "finance guy" (or gal) to support the business aspects of your growth, or a major corporation expanding into new markets, there are times when outside leadership is warranted. However, you must go forward with the understanding that bringing in outside leadership is a culture-changing event, with risks on both sides: many high-profile firms have seen their fortunes sink under new leaders, while according to *Fortune* magazine, new CEOs are three times more likely to get the ax nowadays versus a generation ago. Perhaps the most important survival trait for many organizations as they grow is to assess the cultural compatibility of outside leaders.

This is not to imply that outside management is always a bad thing. The annals of corporate history are filled with companies who grew and prospered under the leadership of new chief executives. And many successful leaders come from outside the ranks of a firm's operations: Southwest Airlines' legendary CEO Herb Kelleher was originally the firm's lawyer, and IBM's dramatic 1990s turnaround was led by Lou Gerstner, a computer industry outsider. But the impact of having a new person at the top—good or bad—underscores how crucial it is to preserve your culture at the highest levels of leadership.

LEADERSHIP AND YOUR CULTURE

Leadership is what mathematicians would call a "necessary but not sufficient condition" for the growth of a corporate culture. Leaders cannot, by themselves, determine corporate culture. They can only influence it. The absence of strong leadership, however, will almost certainly destroy it, and too often this leadership vacuum is fueled by the issues of growth.

Leadership and vision influence your workplace culture more than any other factor. Yet few businesses develop a consistent, values-driven style of leadership. The best ones develop cultures that facilitate the success of their frontline teams, and see management as a tool to empower people to perform at their best. The best create a sense of higher purpose that carries everyone's efforts. At the same time, great leadership does not come naturally, even at the highest levels of an organization. And if you study the impact of leadership on an organization, you will find that every workplace's fundamental conflict between human nature and core values becomes further magnified at the top.

While corporate culture is ultimately the product of every person within an organization, Visionaries are clearly the keepers of this culture. For this reason, the development and preservation of leadership is perhaps the most important survival trait for most businesses. Good organizations know to look beyond their balance sheets and assess the impact of potential leaders' style and vision on their existing cultures. More important, they invest in developing leadership at all levels of the organization, not just at the top. By having the right people in positions of authority, the best work environments build foundations that ultimately self-perpetuate their cultures.

The St. Paul Saints
Fun Is Good

Imagine starting an independent minor league baseball team just miles away from a city that already has a major league franchise. Now imagine having it sell out nearly every game, drawing even bigger crowds than the major league team once in a while. Since debuting in 1993, the St. Paul Saints have managed to attract an average of nearly 6,500 people in the stands every night, while becoming a darling of the national media. In the process, they have become a veritable case study on the impact of creative leadership on a sports franchise.

Created as part of a bold move to start an independent minor league, the Saints are headed by one of the most inventive minds in baseball. Saints founder Mike Veeck is the son of legendary major league baseball owner Bill Veeck, famous for publicity stunts such as putting a midget in the lineup and marrying couples at home plate. Together with an ownership group that included comedy actor Bill Murray, they resurrected a St. Paul, Minnesota, baseball franchise with historical roots that went all the way back to 1903, along with a civic initiative to expand local Midway Stadium to a full-scale 6,500-seat minor league facility. Their intention was to create a competitive hometown team that was separate from the major league farm system controlling most minor league franchises. Their goal was to create an unabashedly good time for everyone who entered the ballpark.

In keeping with the Veeck family tradition, promotions abound at Saints games, ranging from the usual cap giveaways all the way to Phobia Night and Battle of the Sexes night. A group of nuns gives massages in the stands, the team's mascot (a pig) trots balls to home plate, and corporate sponsors host a range of publicity stunts between innings. And some promotions are on an even grander scale—in last season's Saint for a Summer promotion, law student Nick Cichowicz was moved into a mobile home inside Midway Stadium at the beginning of the season with a computer, an Internet connection, a $5,000 debit card, and the understanding that he was not allowed to leave the stadium for the rest of the season. He posted regular e-mail updates to the Saints Web site during the summer, served as a scoreboard operator during games, and even had women vying for a date with him one game night in a Be Nick's Chick promotion—and ultimately won the $5,000 prize for persevering for the entire season.

Amid the fun and games, there is also a pretty good baseball team on the field. The Saints have made the playoffs in all but two years of its eight-year existence, and have been league champions three times to date. They have also been the home of comeback attempts from baseball greats such as World Series hero Jack Morris, as well as the 1997 debut of pitcher Ila Borders, the first female to play regularly for a professional baseball team. (Midway through the season, she also became the first female player to be traded, after posting an undistinguished 7.50 earned run average.) And unlike in the major leagues, there is a very high level of accessibility between players and fans.

The team has been profitable every year of its existence, and its high profile in the community has attracted an unusual level of corporate sponsorship, totaling nearly 40 percent of its revenue, which fuels many of their promotions. And to say that fans are committed is an understatement. In addition to filling the ballpark to capacity every night, the fans even overwhelmingly vetoed having a new stadium replace their "home" in a recent survey. In an era when other independent leagues have come and gone, the entire Northern League has become a success story, and while the St. Paul Saints are among the top 10 percent of minor league franchises in annual attendance, other teams in their own league now draw similar numbers as well.

More than anything, the success of the St. Paul Saints demonstrates the impact of good leadership at several levels. First, in much the same way as his late father Bill Veeck turned around the fortunes of several major league teams by shrewd marketing, Saints owner Mike Veeck has shown that the same principles scale downward into smaller markets, beyond the reach of the major leagues. (And in a fitting turnabout, he remains in considerable demand as a marketing consultant to major league baseball teams.) Second, by involving the fans in business decisions like whether to build a new stadium or hold promotions, the Saints create a strong sense of customer loyalty. Finally, beneath all the fun and games is a carefully maintained brand identity that casts this independent baseball franchise as a community phenomenon, whose family entertainment value has grown beyond the game itself. Their omnipresent motto "Fun is good" sums up both the core values behind an irreverent baseball franchise that has captured the heart of its community for nearly a decade and counting.

9

Why Do Corporate Cultures Fail?

It would be very convenient to divide the world into good cultures and bad cultures, and then make the case that the good ones succeed and the bad ones fail. Unfortunately, the world isn't quite that simple. At the same time, some important parallels can be drawn between your cultural values and your level of success.

First of all, bad cultures often *do* fail. If you look critically at the core values mentioned in the previous chapters, nearly all of us can think of businesses who didn't follow them, and paid a price for it—either by ceasing operations entirely or by becoming one of the many "walking wounded" who limp along with high turnover, low morale, and no idea why they can't be more successful. Most important, they often miss out on the potential that sometimes lies untapped in their own people.

But so-called good cultures can fail as well. And there are some interesting and subtle reasons why they do. Sometimes the causes are as simple as the market itself. For example, a great culture that runs a railroad may not make the leap to the jet age. Or economics catch up with them, as with one firm whose expenditures on quality initiatives contributed to their folding shortly after winning the coveted Malcolm Baldridge quality award. And other reasons can ensnare strong cultures, because of their very nature.

Understanding these reasons can help good organizations look beyond their cultural values and stay fresh and competitive in years to come.

WHY STRONG CULTURES ALONE ARE NO GUARANTEE OF SUCCESS

What do Wang Laboratories, People Express Airlines, and Data General all have in common? Two things. Each was once held up as a paragon of corporate culture 20 years ago. And none of them exists today. They all experienced strong growth that was driven by clear fundamental values—in fact, two of them had books published about their management philosophies—but each later stumbled in the marketplace in the years to come, and all were eventually acquired by other companies.

A landmark 1992 research study by John Kotter and James Hesket looked in detail at how business cultures that once worked well can turn against the best interests of your organization, as well as the core traits that drive long-term successful cultures. In their book *Corporate Culture and Performance,* they came to the surprising conclusion that strong corporate cultures alone do *not* correlate with success in the marketplace. Instead, they found that cultures that combine strong values with adaptability to a changing marketplace are the ones that are highly successful. They put numbers to these conclusions: over a study period of more than a decade, companies with these successful cultures had more than 4 times the revenue growth, 7 times the employment growth, and 12 times the stock price growth of those that did not.

Many firms recognized in the past for their corporate cultures have stumbled in the marketplace in subsequent years. And for many weaker organizations, success often leads them to collapse under the weight of the culture they began with. Some of the factors that lead these once-successful cultures to fail include the following:

The Perils of Success

When I was once part of a struggling software start-up, a very high level of commitment and teamwork carried us through to sudden market success.

But that success brought with it a whole new set of challenges, including management power struggles, competitive pressures, and sharp disagreements on new product directions. The company survived these challenges, and remains very strong today as part of a much larger corporation. But they were neither easy, nor bloodless, for the people who first set out to establish this company and its culture.

Jet aircraft need full power to climb, and then need to throttle back and fly efficiently at cruising altitude. In a similar manner, a business must go through a predictable evolution of its culture during the phases of its life cycle. The values of a highly entrepreneurial organization—teamwork, self-sacrifice, and making do with scarce resources—must eventually grow to become those of an organization with an established position in its marketplace. As you succeed, you must plan to run on excellence rather than on adrenaline. Often this means shifting your thinking from the urgency of the present to the needs of the future.

In cases like these, early-stage decisions in successful businesses—and once again, the conflict between human nature and core values—set the stage for later growth and survival. While this evolution may be clear for new businesses, it is no less of an imperative for established firms that find themselves in a changing market, as evidenced by the recent demise of two major European airlines.

SWISSAIR AND SABENA—GROUNDED BY COMPETITION

Swissair and Sabena were two airlines that for decades were seen as the epitomes of the European flag carrier. Once heavily subsidized by their respective governments in Switzerland and Belgium, they flourished under the highly regulated environment of air transport in Europe. Routes and carriers were tightly controlled, and fares were sometimes so high that it was theoretically cheaper to fly between two nearby European cities via New York. Within this environment, both carriers focused successfully on fostering their home countries' reputation for quality and reliability.

By early 2002 each of these airlines had ceased operations, the result of a complex web of financial and competitive factors ranging from overexpansion to reduced passenger traffic following the September 11 terrorist attacks in the United States. At a deeper level, the privatization of European state airlines in recent years forced what were once heavily bureaucratic organizations to cope with the realities of making a profit in an increasingly competitive air travel market. Today, both carriers have had their operations taken over by smaller airlines that were once their subsidiaries.

One rock star's manager once noted in a television interview that he had seen many recording artists survive failure, but few if any survive success. In much the same way, business success brings its own unique set of challenges, and while they may seem like nice problems to have to those on the outside, they must be understood and managed for good cultures to survive in the long term.

Survivor Bias

Human nature tells us to look at who is successful and learn from what they do. But sometimes success mirrors short-lived trends that don't translate well to the future. Thus, we must look at the best practices of companies within their cultural context, and be aware that these practices—like human beings—evolve over time.

One good example of this is a political one. When Richard Nixon resigned in disgrace as president of the United States during the Watergate scandal of the 1970s, America wanted someone with a squeaky-clean reputation in the Oval Office and elected Jimmy Carter. Four years later, on the heels of the Iran hostage crisis, Americans wanted a president who didn't appear weak and elected Ronald Reagan. Chances are very good that Reagan could not have been elected at the start of Carter's era, given the mood of the country, just as the converse became true four years later. This is why you can never define the traits behind an ideal president for all time.

The same phenomenon is true for corporate cultures. For example, many "lifetime employment and a pension" workplaces of the 20th century became seen as hidebound, change-resistant bureaucracies by century's end, with long-term employees of these firms sometimes derisively referred to as "dinosaurs." Conversely, after the dot-com implosion of 2000 and beyond, the allure of hot, risk-taking, high-growth cultures started to pale, and stable firms once again began to look more attractive. So the people who held up the Sears of the 1950s and the dot-coms of the 1990s as examples of great corporate culture are both partially right and partially wrong. Each would be more accurate if they saw some core traits with strengths that are timeless and others that depend on the surrounding culture of the time. This is why no research study, no matter how far back it extends, will ever fully prescribe an accurate road map for businesses of the future.

Business Fortunes

If you made hula hoops in the 1950s, pet rocks in the 1970s, or launched an advertiser-supported Web portal site in the 1990s, you might have felt that your corporate culture—whatever it was—was a very successful one. More to the point, if you were a successful Fortune 500 company during these periods, you would probably find that the battle between the forces of inertia and the forces of changes was often won by inertia. In any of these cases, business has a life of its own. Trends come and go, fads appear and disappear, and even some long-standing traditions bite the dust at any given point in time.

If you have a culture that is built around excellence in a particular product or service, therefore, your fortunes depend on both your culture *and* the fate of that product or service. And for most businesses, this is a process that never ends, as illustrated by the fortunes of one of America's major grocery chains.

A&P—A CONSTANT EVOLUTION IN MARKET IDENTITY

Many people in the northeastern United States have shopped at **A&P** supermarkets, but few of them know what A&P stands for: the Great Atlantic &

Pacific Tea Company. And as the name implies, it began life in the 1800s as a tea retailer, eliminating the middleman to drastically lower the price of tea to consumers. Soon after the turn of the 20th century, it quickly expanded into the grocery business by pioneering cash-and-carry "economy" stores offering lower prices than the competition. In the 1930s, many of these stores were closed as the company turned its focus towards the growing trends of large-scale supermarkets. By 1950, its revenues were second only to General Motors in the United States.

In the decades since, fierce competition has forced A&P to constantly reexamine its strategy, with the growth of competing superstores, all-encompassing "big box" retailers such as Wal-Mart, and niche-market food stores. After recent decades of ups and downs, and now the parent firm of numerous regional markets such as Kohl's, Waldbaum's, and Farmer Jack, it is once again expanding behind a new technology infrastructure and a renewed push into new markets—and as of this writing, its $10 billion annual revenues are once again moving upwards.

The lesson in stories like these is the need for constant reinvention—the A&P of 1850 could not survive forever as a tea company, nor as the economy grocer of 1915, the supermarket chain of 1930, the corporate behemoth of 1950, or the aging retailer of the 1980s. And these changes that are required to move from one phase to the next can be massive in scope. For example, a half an hour's drive from my hometown is a former A&P distribution center that covers several city blocks and nearly two million square feet, which has been shuttered for well over a decade. But the company continues to flourish into its third century, and 20 years from now, chances are that it will still be changing once again—or pay the price for not doing so. In a similar manner, every business culture must continually hold up its values and business practices against the competitive realities of the world that it operates in.

Cultural Myopia

Good cultures often lead to growth and success. But that same success can also blind a culture to the realities of its business. It is often seductive to feel that your great culture and its current success will support poorly-thought-out business directions, allow you to ignore competition, or fuel unsustainable growth. In reality, no business is exempt from either the competitive jungle or the laws of supply and demand.

J. PETERMAN AND THE LIMITS OF GROWTH

J. Peterman was not only a successful catalog clothing retailer, but one of the cultural icons of the 1990s. His purple-prose catalogs conjured up images of a mid-20th century world of international travel, literary figures, and intrigue, with shirts inspired by the great Gatsby, caftans designed for Chinese empresses, and leather diplomatic pouches. His company eventually became part of a running satire on the hit television show *Seinfeld* (where primary character Elaine was cast as one of his employees), while the company he started for $500 selling one coat grew to become a $75-million-per-year empire with 13 stores and a 100-page catalog.

By the end of the 1990s, however, overexpansion and cash-flow problems caught up with J. Peterman. Just like many dot-com companies of the era, his venture capital–backed dreams of a billion-dollar-plus empire led to a rate of growth that couldn't be sustained by paying customers, and it crashed and burned in a 1999 bankruptcy. As Peterman himself later noted in a *Time* magazine interview, "With venture capital, no one's interested in slow development." Today, he is back once again with a slimmed-down catalog and an online storefront, as well as a book and campus lectures examining his earlier rise and fall.

These cultural blind spots are not just limited to business factors; sometimes they extend to the relevance of the culture itself. For example, IBM's strict business dress code conveyed an image of professionalism decades ago, but later it made employees appear to be stuffy suits in an era of young, hip innovators, and IBM eventually reinvented itself to fit the times. Similarly, the post–World War II era was marked by the rise of large paternalistic workplaces with layers of middle management, employing a generation that craved stability and family values above all else. Some of these firms evolved nicely into a business landscape that is now leaner and more competitive, while others became blind to their own obsolescence. Successful firms who are in for the long haul understand that they must constantly reexamine who they are and fine-tune their values to suit the times they live and compete in.

It is a paradox to many people that you can fail because you are good. But the reality of business, and of life, is that each level of success brings a fresh set of challenges to face and expectations to meet. Most sandlot baseball players, for instance, dream of making the major leagues, but when Boston Red Sox first baseman Bill Buckner let a routine ground ball roll between his legs during the 1986 World Series, and his team's hopes for a title roll away with it, the memories of that one mistake overshadowed a brilliant career from that day on. In much the same way, great cultures run the risk of not meeting the expectations set for themselves, in a world that may dub one firm a billion-dollar-a-year failure and another a million-dollar-a-year success. In the long term, the fate of both hinge on how their cultures evolve over time, in a world that ultimately requires every organization to constantly reexamine itself.

SUCCESS, FAILURE, AND YOUR CULTURE

While it is true that good cultures can fail, it is even truer that the lack of a good culture is a strong factor against your success. In fact, cultural issues are the key factors in many business failures, if not most. For example, my experiences with two particular computer manufacturers stand out as microcosms of the cultures behind them and their consequences.

TWO COMPUTERS, AND
TWO CORPORATE CULTURES

In the early 1990s, I purchased a desktop system from Dell. It ran flawlessly for years, and I rarely had to call for service. When I did, the response was nothing short of incredible. I was always connected quickly to polite, knowledgeable people who addressed me by name and resolved my problems right away. One weekend, trying to install a new disk drive, a technician patiently guided me through which jumpers to connect and settings to change—at 2 AM on a Sunday morning. Another time, when my mouse malfunctioned, I was shipped a replacement via a delivery service that promptly went on strike the next day. Another phone call, and a second mouse was immediately on its way—this time via FedEx, and compliments of Dell.

Years later, I purchased a computer from another vendor. It was dead on arrival when I first brought it home, and trying to get it fixed involved an unsuccessful two-day marathon of being passed from one snippy person to another. After finally making myself a happy customer by returning my system to the store for a replacement, a monotonal telemarketer from their "quality team" called me to survey how I would rate my service experience. (The answers I gave are best left to the reader's imagination.) Later, my technical support experiences were equally bad, including one Kafkaesque incident where their advice left my system completely nonfunctional, and I was then told that I couldn't speak to them about it without opening (and paying for) another support incident.

Some people might see these experiences as a simple case of good versus bad service, but a chance encounter later confirmed that the second company's culture made good service nearly impossible. One day I was teaching a corporate training workshop and one of the students happened to mention that she used to be a supervisor at this second computer firm's technical support center. I couldn't resist asking what it was like to work there. Her eyes rolled skyward, and she slowly shook her head. She then described a tale where management had little respect for people on the front lines, departments wouldn't communicate with each other, and turnover was off the charts. She even voiced a perception that conflicts between department heads of different nationalities fueled their refusal to cooperate with each other.

Now, let's fast-forward from my own experiences to the behavior of the marketplace. Dell Computer has become one of the legendary success stories of the technology industry. Growing at healthy double-digit rates for much of the past decade to current revenues of more than $30 billion per year as of this writing, it has recently become the world's largest computer manufacturer. Conversely, the other computer firm eventually went down in flames with substantial losses, despite being in the middle of one of the hottest growth periods of personal computing.

For both of these computer firms, you could argue that their success or failure had as much to do with their basic stance towards life as it did with their specific business decisions. And they are far from alone. If you scratch the surface of many business fortunes, you will find similar factors at work. For most organizations, you could group their basic values behind their decision making and their culture into one of the following categories.

Good Values

Decisions are made with values that resonate with employees, customers, and the marketplace.

No Values

Decisions are made by human nature.

Old Values

Decisions are made with values that have not changed to reflect current realities.

Wrong Values

Decisions are made with values that are dysfunctional for employees, customers, and the marketplace.

Of course, as discussed in the previous section, your business culture is rarely if ever the sole ingredient in your success. Perhaps the most accurate view is that it is one of the more important legs of a three-legged stool, where the other legs are the products and services you sell, and your approach to the market. When one of these legs gets out of balance from the other, the results can be far from optimal, no matter how great your culture is.

SATURN—A GREAT CULTURE AND A TINY MARKET SHARE

The Saturn division of General Motors has been widely praised as an example of good corporate citizenship, ranging from its innovative union contracts to the way it sells and services its vehicles. Saturn cars have a fixed sticker price, there is no haggling, and its salespeople are salaried "consultants" who practice a low-pressure, informational approach to sales. At one point, one of its television commercials showed a dealership's entire sales team applauding as a young woman was given the keys to her first new car, while an earlier ad documented the true story of a Saturn dealer flying someone to Alaska to replace a car seat.

All these good vibes helped Saturn capture a great deal of mind-share in the corporate press throughout the 1990s, but this never translated to a substantial market share in the competitive automotive marketplace. The cars themselves suffered from lukewarm reviews, fair-to-middling styling, and early problems such as excessive road noise. Worse yet, parent company GM's reluctance to approve new models caused it to react too slowly to the decline of small cars and a growing appetite for models such as sport-utility vehicles. Today, Saturn's market share languishes at 1.4 percent, and GM is currently pumping $1.5 billion into the company in an effort to revive its fortunes.

Conversely, some companies let their cultural values take a backseat to doing whatever it takes to succeed, and then worry about building their long-term culture once this happens. While this approach doesn't always make for heartwarming stories in the business press, sometimes it does work.

NICE GUYS DON'T ALWAYS FINISH FIRST

In the 1980s, I worked in a niche market of the software industry that was populated by a small, tight-knit fraternity of entrepreneurs, who sold products based on their technical merits. Then a new firm came along who changed the rules of its whole marketing game. The firm's salespeople were slick, aggressive, and bold. They often bypassed the engineers who used these products, making their pitches directly to the financial decision makers in the corner offices. And they weren't at all afraid to "go negative" in pursuit of the sale, bad-mouthing competitors or pressuring undecided prospects. If a sale was at risk on technical grounds, it was not unusual for the sales staff to even call an engineer's manager and question the engineer's competence, often taking advantage of the boss's own technical ignorance.

Few people would have characterized this company as a relaxed place to work during its early years. There were long hours, high pressure, and an ultimatum to "produce or else" in both the technical and sales arenas. But it succeeded far beyond anyone's wildest expectations, becoming one of the industry success stories of the decade. Today, its sales approach has been toned down somewhat from its early days. But the company has survived and prospered through good times, bad times, and changing markets, and remains at the top of its game today.

In a similar vein, during the Internet explosion of the 1990s, some of the major online services seemed to be positioning themselves as the gold standard for poor service. It was not unusual to find long delays, indifferent support technicians, and poor responses to problems. Yet some of these firms who were publicly blasted for poor service cultures eventually grew to dominate their markets, often at the expense of other firms who did a much better job of treating their customers.

In cases like these, where it seems like some companies succeed and flourish despite the feelings of their customers and their employees, other factors are usually at work. These include better products, better services, a more competitive price point, or market leadership in a new technology area. Moreover, their seeming "anticultures" do not always translate well to other environments. For example, in the engineering software example mentioned previously, many firms soon tried to mimic the aggressive "frat boy" selling model of their newfound competitor—and most of them fell on their faces in short order. By comparison, this competitor paired its aggressiveness with a truly groundbreaking product that was light-years ahead of its competition.

Perhaps most telling is that as companies like these succeed in the marketplace, their cultures often improve with the growth of the company, perhaps as a result of lessons driven by their own success. The key difference between these firms and those whose values fail them is that they often evolve over time and build on their successes by developing a more sustainable, lasting culture.

Whichever paths an organization takes to its success, most of those that succeed eventually do develop a set of unique values that define their competitive posture. And for those that succeed for the long term, these values generally include traits such as adaptability, outward vision, and continuous learning about themselves and the world around them. They display a keen sensitivity to changes in their workforce, their customer base, and society itself. Perhaps most important, they have a clear sense of who they are, and they combine that with an equally clear sense of how to make a profit. They understand that success is a continuous and never-ending process, driven both by the practicalities of business life and the underlying principles that guide them.

KEEPING A STRONG CULTURE ALIVE

Some cultures ultimately fail because they simply are bad. For example, I once had repeated credit problems with one retail chain, because of computer problems and human error on its part. When mentioning this in passing to one of its store clerks one day, the clerk erupted into a tirade about how she had similar credit problems with the store, and how indifferent and bureaucratic it was towards its own employees. Not long afterwards, the company was ensnared in a major auto repair fraud scandal. By the time the company finally declared bankruptcy and disappeared from the retail landscape, it seemed like a very dysfunctional organization was being put out of its misery.

But even the best of cultures can ill afford to rest on their laurels. No organization is immune from external forces such as market pressures, or internal ones such as changes of leadership. And no corporate culture guarantees your success in the future. No single organization in existence today can afford to stop listening to both its employees and the marketplace, and, as a result, every business culture requires constant fine-tuning to survive and flourish.

At the same time, clearly your values, and not your business processes, still determine how successful your organization will be. In a sense, these cultural values have an influence similar to that of your own personal values. People with high integrity, good interpersonal skills, and strong work ethics tend to get ahead, for example, even if there is no guarantee against factors such as poor career choices or economic problems. And for most people, these values have much more to do with their success than external factors such as degrees or work experience. The same is no less true of an organization. And while no corporate culture represents an ironclad guarantee against failure, the right core values still remain the biggest factors in your success.

10

Cultural Due Diligence
Mergers, Acquisitions, and
Other Growth Strategies

F**rom the smallest businesses to** the world's largest corporate titans, the search for synergy often leads people to seek new markets and new partners. The vast majority of these efforts are driven by business factors, but according to numerous experts, they succeed or fail more often because of cultural factors than for any other reason. As a result, the organization that understands its core values is much more likely to reach the kind of growth and success that nearly all businesses seek.

Kenneth Smith, author of a recent Mercer Management Consulting report on acquisitions, notes bluntly that most corporate mergers end in failure. Moreover, they usually do so because of what happens after the deal is consummated, particularly for the people on the inside. According to Smith, "Mishandling the consequences of a merger on employees can literally be a deal breaker, because it can irretrievably destroy value." Conversely, corporate relationships that start from a good culture fit have the potential to add value to employees, shareholders, and customers alike.

Every successful business faces three critical risk points as it seeks to expand its operations:

1. Growth by merger or acquisition

2. Crossing the international border
3. Expansion into new markets

Each of them presents unique opportunities and a corresponding set of risks that need to be understood and managed to succeed. By understanding the cultural implications behind each of these paths, organizations gain a much better chance to survive and flourish in the long term, whatever direction their growth takes them.

CULTURE AND GROWTH BY ACQUISITION

Competition inevitably fuels consolidation. If you have 400 one-acre farms, each with their own tractors, barns, and silos, they cannot be as efficient as larger operations that can pool their resources. And businesses often complement each other: if you sell ice cream and your neighbor sells sandwiches, together you may have the seeds of a successful restaurant, or a major restaurant chain. As businesses rise to the top of their industries, it is rare to find a leading firm that hasn't eventually partnered with other businesses to fuel its growth. At the same time, the wrong kinds of mergers have often weakened an organization, and in some cases even been the death knell for once-strong companies. How an organization manages growth by acquisition is often the defining moment for its long-term culture, as was the case in recent years at Delta Airlines.

DELTA AIRLINES—NEW PARTNERS, CHANGING CULTURES

The Delta Airlines of the 1980s was, by all accounts, a great company to work for. It had a long-standing no-layoff policy, its customer satisfaction ratings were best-of-class, and it inspired such loyalty among its employees that many of them voluntarily chipped in 2 percent of their salaries to purchase the company a brand-new, paid-in-full 767 jetliner—a nearly $50-million thank-you for protecting their jobs in a tough economic climate. By the time Delta was pro-filed in the 1982 best-seller *In Search of Excellence,* it was celebrated as a shining example of corporate paternalism.

But Delta also was still a relatively small and regional carrier in a market that was starting to consolidate. So, in 1987, it merged with Western Airlines, and in 1991, it became a major global player by acquiring the transatlantic routes of bankrupt Pan American Airways. Suddenly, it found itself adding the staff of two traditional airlines, which had traditional "us versus them" labor relations, to its seniority lists. And more changes were on the horizon: three years later, in 1994, nearly 15,000 positions were eliminated, and in 1996, substantial concessions were negotiated from its pilots' union. Instead of wearing "Spirit of Delta" but-tons celebrating the company's employee-paid jetliner of a decade ago, some employees now angrily wore buttons proclaiming "So Be It," taken from one CEO's comment about how his cost-cutting measures would cause morale and service quality to plummet. Employee relations have since improved in recent years under a subsequent change of leadership, but as of this writing, the com-pany—currently the world's third largest air carrier—has still just narrowly dodged its first strike.

The urge to merge is strong: in 1998, more than 23,000 organizations worldwide were involved in acquisitions with a net worth of over $2.3 tril-lion. And it has grown stronger over time, as merger activity grew expo-nentially during the junk-bond financing era of the 1980s and continued beyond the corporate reengineering years of the 1990s. But change is never easy, and few changes are as anxiety provoking as watching someone take over the organization that provides your livelihood. And beyond the core fear of seeing one's job disappear or change drastically, there are deeper quality-of-life issues involved with partnering with another company. When a freewheeling, open working environment suddenly becomes managed by a buttoned-down, govern-from-the-top organization—or vice versa—it has the potential to change the very things that made the merger attractive in the first place.

SNAPPLE AND QUAKER OATS—THE MERGER THAT LOST MORE THAN A BILLION DOLLARS

Snapple was an upstart company whose all-natural beverages, combined with a unique marketing approach, made it first a cult favorite and then a major national brand. Started in 1972 by two health food store owners, Snapple produced flavored iced teas and juice drinks that soon epitomized the New Age and gained the rousing endorsement of personalities such as radio shock-jock Howard Stern, who became a commercial pitchman for the company. Snapple's own quirky advertising featured "the Snapple Lady" reading letters from customers, and by 1994 the company was receiving more than 20 boxes of fan mail per month from people who loved its products. Behind this public image was a tightly knit New York–area company with a laid-back management style and a network of independent regional distributors.

By the early 1990s, Snapple attracted the attention of **Quaker Oats,** who purchased the company for a staggering $1.7 billion. Quaker promptly fired the Snapple Lady (who "didn't fit their new image"), severed the drinks' advertising ties with Howard Stern, replaced the old distribution model with Quaker's existing channels, and perhaps most important, brought in a new layer of "professional management." Snapple seemingly lost its identity in the marketplace from that point on. Sales floundered, market share declined, and just two years later the company was sold again for $300 million, less than 20 percent of its original purchase price.

While the Quaker-Snapple marriage ranks as one of the most spectacular failed mergers in recent corporate history, with its $1.4 billion loss, it has an interesting postscript. Its new owner Triarc Beverage brought in an industry-savvy CEO, instituted a very open level of communication with the firm's employees, and even rehired the original Snapple Lady (explaining in its new ads that she had been stranded on a desert island). It also paired Snapple as part of a business unit with other niche-market beverages such as RC Cola and Stewart's Sodas, rather than forcing Snapple into the mainstream. The revived Snapple has performed very well in the marketplace in recent years, and was recently sold again to Cadbury-Schweppes—who vows to maintain the firm's independence—for a respectable $1.4 billion.

Whenever a major new partner becomes part of your business plans, you often move from the incremental growth of your own efforts to the sudden growth of adding significant head count, market share, and production capacity. Thus, the previous cultures of both the acquirer and the acquired can change rapidly, and sometimes mercilessly. Above all, it is becoming clear that the balance sheet of companies that grow by acquisition is ultimately driven by the human element—in particular, the day-to-day work life of employees who remain.

Sometimes a merger works out well for all concerned. For example, when The CBORD Group acquired the interests of a smaller software company serving catering operations, both parties benefited immediately. The smaller firm suddenly gained the marketing muscle and 24-hour customer support operations of a larger software company, with no involuntary personnel departures, while CBORD immediately gained thousands of new customers and an entrée into an entry-level market. On a broader scale, marriages between complementary businesses have brought growth, infrastructure, and a consistent service culture to many firms who were once isolated fiefdoms.

On the other hand, the wrong kind of merger can kill a culture, and sometimes take the company with it. When Daisy Systems, one of the major players in computer-aided design (CAD) software, decided to launch a hostile takeover of rival Cadnetix in 1989, it succeeded. Despite a hot market for electronic design software, the merged company soon went bankrupt. Even in less dramatic cases, the wounds can be lasting. According to estimations by *Fortune* magazine, recent acquisitions by insurance company Conseco and toymaker Mattel have wiped out more than $20 billion from their combined market capitalization.

The sad truth is that nearly two-thirds of corporate mergers do not work out as well as expected, even in the short term, and the reasons often have little to do with business issues. In the Mercer Consulting Group's study, figures show that even leveraged buyouts (which often lack the business synergies of other mergers) do better than merged companies taken as a whole. In explanation, they state bluntly that many of these failures are caused by not conducting the same kind of "due diligence" on the culture, structure, and processes of an acquisition target as they do on the financial balance sheet. Conversely, when culture assessment becomes part of the acquisition process, the results can be very strong for both parties, as was the case when Southwest Airlines merged with smaller carrier Morris Air in 1994.

A MARRIAGE OF LIKE-MINDED CULTURES

When Southwest Airlines decided to acquire Salt Lake City–based charter carrier **Morris Air** to expand its coverage of the West Coast market, it spent a full two months evaluating how the cultures of the two companies would "fit" prior to consummating the $134-million deal in early 1994. In this case, it had learned from experience: much earlier in its history, its $60-million acquisition of rival Muse Air from former president Lamar Muse never performed up to expectations, and its assets were sold less than two years later.

By comparison, the Morris acquisition was a case of imitation being the sincerest form of flattery. The 21-jet carrier was founded in 1984 to emulate the Southwest Airlines model of low-fare, low-cost service, and shared both a similar management culture and a common aircraft type—the Boeing 737. The deal, which was in fact initiated by Morris Air founder June Morris, combined two airlines with similar philosophies and nonoverlapping routes into an even stronger national carrier. The merger was well received overall by Morris's 2,000 employees, many of whom started getting unsolicited "welcome aboard" cards and gifts from Southwest employees as soon as the merger was announced.

In cases where there is a strong business case for merging, but not a close match of culture, it makes sense to consider the retention and productivity impact of an "arranged marriage." In some cases, the subsequent loss of management and professional talent from an ill-advised merger scuttle the hopes and plans that both parties brought to the negotiating table. Sometimes, the most important ingredient in merging two cultures is to respect the unique differences between each organization, and leverage these differences to help people from each business entity play to their strengths.

Mergers and acquisitions, or "M&A" as they are known in the trade, serve as a prime example of how intangible aspects such as corporate culture can hold sway over billions of dollars and thousands of careers. When done well, they have the potential to grow markets, build on complementary strengths, and eliminate inefficiency. But because they involve human beings, it is impossible to predict their success on a balance sheet solely through tangible factors such as infrastructure, head count, or market share. What ultimately matters in an acquisition is what happens in the hearts and minds of the people who remain with the new organization, and what culture these formerly distinct entities choose to build while moving forward. Some of the key cultural issues that must to be assessed in planning for these partnerships include the following:

Management Style

Organizations vary in their personalities, just like people do. One successful organization may have an entirely different set of values from another one, and dysfunctional cultures can sabotage good ones when the two are brought into contact. Therefore, one of the most important cultural factors to assess in a business partner is the compatibility of your respective leadership styles. A company's style of management has a ripple effect on every facet of daily business operations, from what kinds of people have been hired all the way to policies and procedures.

Thus, when two organizations merge, the impact of a new leadership culture must be thought through in advance, down to the operations level. Sometimes changes in leadership styles are desirable: the right infusion of new leadership can make good companies great, or bring a lasting culture to what were formerly just undifferentiated products and services. But the objectives must be clear ahead of time, and the resulting management culture must ultimately fit both partners to succeed in the long run.

Underlying Philosophy

Mergers and acquisitions bring the respective business philosophies of new partners into sharp focus, and these values must be in synch between an organization and its new leadership. For example, when Wegmans Food Stores acquired fellow Rochester, New York–based home improvement chain Chase-Pitkin in the 1970s, the result was a marriage of two diverse "big box" retailers who developed a common ethic of consistent service quality, modern facilities, and strong employee career paths as both grew and prospered. (Fittingly, Chase-Pitkin itself was formed by a merger of a different sort in the mid-1800s, when founder Lewis Chase's daughter married local society figure William Pitkin and put him in charge of their nursery operations.) Conversely, the tension between new leadership and "that's how we've always done things here" can sabotage the best efforts at business synergy, unless core workplace beliefs on both sides are frankly assessed and discussed ahead of time.

Communication Style

One of the culture changes that people are most sensitive to is the flow of information. Good communication, in particular, is crucial during that sensitive period when two organizations first join forces. Being frank with information and sharing your long-term game plan clearly can mean the difference between chaos and acceptance during the transition to new leadership and beyond.

In the short term, perhaps the most important cultural factor to understand and manage is the fallout from the merger itself. Partnering with a new firm is a period of great anxiety and uncertainty for the acquired company, even under the best of circumstances. People will often assume the worst in an uncertain situation, particularly when their livelihoods are at stake in a corporate merger. Companies who take over other firms are at great risk of losing the acquired firm's best talent, particularly those people who have options to go elsewhere, while retaining a firm's more marginal performers. Even a friendly merger that is revenue-neutral and designed to retain people's jobs runs the risk of changing the resulting mix of talent involved.

WE MERGED, AND THEY LEFT

I was once part of a software firm whose management acquired a smaller technology firm, whose product complemented its own product line very well. There was one hitch, however. Immediately following the merger, nearly all the acquired firm's management left unexpectedly to start a new venture of their own. After some frantic scrambling, this company's product and staff were eventually integrated within our company, but not without the need to build a new management team from within our own firm's resources.

In the longer term, how well you communicate at all levels becomes an important part of the new culture moving forward. Thus, a business partnership represents a new opportunity for better sharing of information, which, in turn, can help new ownership represent a culture change for the better in the eyes of your employees.

Business Practices

Perhaps the greatest long-term fear when a workplace has new leadership and takes on the business identity of its new partner is that of losing what worked well in the past. Therefore, it is critical to assess what business traditions have worked well in the past with your new partner, and which ones should be assimilated into the new culture—particularly when you have a strong culture to begin with, as was the case with superpremium ice cream maker and corporate culture icon Ben & Jerry's Homemade, Inc.

BEN & JERRY'S—CHERRY GARCIA
MEETS CORPORATE LIFE

When British conglomerate Unilever decided to purchase ice cream icon **Ben & Jerry's Homemade, Inc.,** perhaps one of the most important things that it did was to leave Ben & Jerry's culture alone. Because the ice cream company was a socially conscious firm that donated 7.5 percent of its profits to charity and supported "green" causes, there was a great deal of concern about what might change as a result of being taken over by a major corporation. Nearly two years past its spring 2000 acquisition, Ben & Jerry's still continues to maintain its most important traditions. Its charitable arm, for instance, The Ben & Jerry's Foundation, still operates independently of the company, which means that it occasionally donates to causes that protest against corporations such as Unilever. And new Ben & Jerry's CEO Yves Couette, a longtime Unilever veteran, has shed his pinstripes for the egalitarian casual garb of his new workplace. Most important, its hip product image and product quality remain unchanged. But new corporate ownership has brought in aggressive sales goals, expansion into new markets, and increased profit levels as of this writing.

Nearly all these factors could be summed up under the heading of "cultural due diligence." The term borrows from the financial due diligence that is part of any merger or acquisition, when the acquiring firm pores over the books and balance sheets of the company it is acquiring to assess its financial health. No one would ever think of moving forward with a merger without this detailed financial check, but if it did the same for assessing a partner's business culture, it would get to examine factors that often loom far larger in the success of a new partnership. By adding this cultural due diligence to your own process for growth by acquisition, you gain a substantial competitive advantage over those firms who do not, and in the process, preserve the values that make you successful as you grow.

WHEN CORPORATE CULTURE MEETS INTERNATIONAL CULTURE

One fall in the 1980s, I had the pleasure of teaching at a university in the People's Republic of China at a time when contacts with the West were still relatively rare. Compared with the Iron Curtain stereotypes of China that I had grown up with, I found my Chinese hosts unfailingly friendly, engaging, and interested in my wife and me as people. People on the street who could speak English (or comprehend my broken phrase-book Chinese) would regularly stop us just to talk and discuss each other's cultures, or even invite us for tea. We made many friends during our stay in what was still an economically developing country.

Then, six months later, I visited Taiwan, a place populated by the same ethnic Chinese people, two generations removed from their days on the mainland. It was like night and day. Taiwan was much more of an economic success, with modern skyscrapers, freeways jammed with late-model cars, and visible signs of wealth everywhere. But at a personal level, it felt more like being in Manhattan than in China. I was just another face in the crowd, clerks rushed me along like anyone else in line, and no one wanted to make small talk. I felt like if I had a heart attack in the middle of an intersection, people would just step over me.

In a similar fashion, business styles and corporate cultures can change radically when you cross an international border, or even move within different ethnic and cultural circles in the same nation. These metacultures may date back hundreds or even thousands of years, and may permeate life well beyond the culture of an individual organization. As businesses large and small increasingly serve the world market, one of the most important business partnerships you can build is the marriage between your own corporate culture and the global culture of your customers. But as one of my colleagues found out, working overseas often requires a change in perspective, even at the personal level of the workplace.

IT'S DIFFERENT BEING AN ENGINEER IN GERMANY

A colleague of mine who is an engineering professor discovered the impact of international culture firsthand when he spent a sabbatical working for a German manufacturing firm. Used to the informal working environment of American technology firms, he bristled at having to come in exactly on time, shake hands every morning with each of his coworkers and greet them by name before starting work, and speak when spoken to by managers. As a creative person who frequently burned the midnight oil, it felt strange to him watching the pencils drop and the employees file towards the door precisely at quitting time every day. In time, he came to appreciate the strengths and work ethic of his European colleagues, but he also felt that he could never work there long term—it simply wasn't "him."

So what happens when a company from Europe, Asia, or America goes global and builds or acquires business interests outside its national boundaries? The answer often depends on its sensitivity to international culture as well as corporate culture.

In some cases, a transfer of cultural styles is healthy. When Japanese automaker Honda decided to start manufacturing cars in Ohio, it brought many of its Japanese management concepts to America. The results benefited the local economy, the careers of its American employees, and ultimately the global consumer.

HONDA OF AMERICA—A CULTURE TRANSLATES WELL TO "MADE IN AMERICA"

Honda of America draws nearly all its production management from the ranks of its assembly line, investing nearly a man-week of training in each employee, and sending dozens per year to visit its plants in Japan. Employees are taught many of the parent company's Japanese management concepts, including quality circles, production teams, and employee involvement in decisions on the assembly line. The result is a manufacturing operation that turned the Honda Accord into the best-selling American car by the late 1980s, and now actually exports thousands of vehicles back to Japan every year. More important, it put the myth of shoddy American automotive manufacturing to rest for good. Since Honda of America Manufacturing first opened its doors in 1982, the quality of its vehicles has been indistinguishable from its Japanese counterparts.

In many ways, Honda can trace its success in America to values that it possessed for decades in Japan, dating back to the days when founder Soichiro Honda defied the Japanese government in the early 1960s to start building automobiles. Its management philosophy revolves around five precepts, publicized to all employees:

1. Proceed always with ambition and youthfulness.
2. Respect sound theory, develop fresh ideas, and make the most effective use of time.
3. Enjoy your work, and always brighten your working atmosphere.
4. Strive constantly for a harmonious flow of work.
5. Be ever mindful of the value of research and endeavor.

The practical application of these principles is a deep respect for the individual and the workplace, values that translated well to the American workforce. This also has led Honda to invest resources in its own key business partners such as suppliers, towards a goal of reducing the cost of building a car in half from levels of the early 1990s. This underlying culture has helped Honda maintain higher profit margins than its much larger competitors, despite being a fraction of their size. More important, it has bankrolled a strong desire for independence amid a merger-swept automotive industry, and thus has preserved the culture that has taken it to its current level of success. Its Japanese values have ultimately given it a competitive advantage on the world stage, to the point where it now sells more automobiles abroad than in its native Japan.

McDonald's is another example of importing a culture successfully. Its restaurants are a ubiquitous presence in major cities around the world, and its international sites are among the company's top performers. (Its busiest restaurant, in Moscow, drew 30,000 people on opening day.) McDonald's always accounts for local preferences when opening a restaurant: in France, for example, its Big Mac sandwich uses a blue-cheese style sauce rather than the standard American dressing, and in many Muslim countries its beef is produced according to strict halal standards. Once, during a visit to Hong Kong, I asked a group of local residents whether they ate at McDonald's for the same reason I did—because it was a quick, inexpensive meal—or because it was an authentic taste of American culture. The unequivocal answer from everyone was "Both!"

In other cases, the culture doesn't translate. The worst examples of cultural conflict across international borders happen when a traditional command-and-control organization makes decisions at headquarters without the input of local management. The classic example of this is when General Motors marketed its Chevrolet Nova in Mexico, experiencing poor sales, seemingly unaware that *no va* translated literally to *no go* in Spanish. In the context of work life, problems can erupt when corporate culture is overshadowed by national culture, as was the case in a recent transatlantic merger of pharmaceutical giants.

UPJOHN AND PHARMACIA—TWO COUNTRIES, TWO WORKPLACE CULTURES

When American pharmaceutical firm Upjohn merged with Swedish drugmaker **Pharmacia AB,** the merger promised to lift both firms to the top level of their market. But cultural issues dogged the new company from day one: the Europeans resisted efforts at employee drug testing, bristled at the amount of reporting the Americans wanted, and even chafed at Upjohn's policies against drinking and smoking in countries where wine and cigars were staples at work. They resented the Americans' top-down style of management changing their team-oriented culture. Conversely, the Americans found it difficult to accommodate European work styles, which included lengthy summer vacations, in their nonstop competitive environment. Since the merger, the two firms have had to work hard to bridge the culture gap as they became a global operation.

Difficulties aside, we are increasingly becoming a global economy, and it is not unusual for the average American family today to buy fast-food hamburgers from a British company, listen to hit albums on Dutch-owned record labels, and call customer-service centers in the Philippines. According to Virginia Reck of the Kendall Consulting Group, more than 6,000 cross-border mergers and acquisitions take place annually, with a combined value of nearly $300 billion, and the rate of these mergers continues to grow. This means that the process of merging corporate cultures now has a growing side effect of changing global cultures.

EXPANDING INTO NEW MARKETS

When you are very successful at one thing, it is very tempting to presume that this success will translate to other things as well. This argument is particularly compelling when there is a business rationale behind expanding beyond your current market, whether it involves new partners or simply a new direction. But here as well, success in a new marketplace has as much to do with your culture as it does with new products and services. Sometimes it makes sense to expand your core business focus, and sometimes it does not.

THE "SEEMED LIKE A GOOD IDEA AT THE TIME" DEPARTMENT

Remember Bill Blass Chocolates? FedEx's ZapMail fax service? Or how about Allegis, the all-encompassing travel colossus that was hoped for when the parent company of United Airlines acquired car rental giant Hertz and Hilton International in the 1980s? All these great ideas fell victim to the marketplace, and continued to teach us that "brand identity" didn't always guarantee success by diversification. The former two were product efforts that failed quickly, while the latter produced skimpy profit margins and a corporate identity that lasted less than a year, ultimately resulting in the sale of its major nonairline assets. Today, all three of these corporations are tightly focused on their core business areas.

The business world is littered with failed new products and services, with some estimates running as high as an 80 percent failure rate in such areas as new consumer products. At the same time, there are clear cultural traits behind the growth of organizations that expand into new markets successfully. If you examine closely what drives the success of an existing culture into a new market, three key factors are critical.

Know Who You Are

Perhaps the most important factor in looking at a new market is understanding the core concepts that drive your current operations, and examining whether new business areas match your underlying values. The business with a mantra of top-tier service may clash head-on with another one focused on working as efficiently as possible, and the organization that focuses on doing one thing very well may find that its values don't scale upwards to broader areas. As a result, it is important to examine how closely your fundamental beliefs translate to new partners and new business areas. W.L. Gore, of Gore-Tex fame, serves as one good example of expanding in harmony with its core strengths.

W.L. GORE—A SINGLE FOCUS, AND DOZENS OF MARKETS

What do outdoor wear, dental floss, and artificial human arteries have in common? In many cases, materials designed and developed by **W.L. Gore and Associates,** best known to the public for the space-age Gore-Tex fabric that has clad hikers and outdoorsmen for decades. Today, the company holds literally hundreds of product patents, which have spread its core business of fluoropolymer material products to dozens of new markets. Nowadays, many consumers are unaware that this famous outerwear material supplier now manufactures products such as Glide dental floss, Elixir guitar strings, and consumer vacuum cleaner filters. These new markets have boosted Gore's annual revenues to more than $1.4 billion per year, doubling in size since the early 1990s.

In management circles, Gore has long had a reputation as the ultimate decentralized organization. Founder Bill Gore started his company on the basis of a principle known as "the lattice organization," where hierarchy is frowned on, and there is a goal of limiting individual plants to 200 or fewer people. As a result, people whose credentials might have held them back elsewhere often get ahead at Gore, and the freedom to innovate isn't based on rank or pedigree. This billion-dollar-plus conglomerate still functions like an innovative network of small businesses, and can quickly exploit new markets that match with their core business strengths.

As organizations, and as people, we all have a certain "brand identity." In some cases, this identity needs to change with the times and adapt to new markets. In other cases, it makes more sense to stay the course and be true to who you are. For example, in the entertainment industry, more than three generations of children ultimately grew up watching puppeteer Shari Lewis and her cast of characters on television.

SHARI LEWIS—A MESSAGE FOR CHILDREN OF ALL TIME

Puppeteer and ventriloquist Shari Lewis was a fixture in children's television in the 1950s and 1960s, hosting a popular show featuring her sock-puppet Lamb Chop. Together with sidekicks Charlie Horse and Hush Puppy, she taught children to believe in themselves. Her show became a Saturday morning staple for an entire generation, and Lamb Chop became such a cultural icon that the puppet even once testified before hearings in Congress.

In the 1990s, it seemed like a novelty to many people when Lewis resurrected her decades-old Lamb Chop character on public television. But the revived *Lamb Chop's Play-Along* managed to successfully blend her message of individual self-worth with the production effects of the MTV generation, and went on to win five daytime Emmy awards. And at the time of her passing in 1998, her new music education series *Charlie Horse's Music Pizza* was still in production, and won yet another posthumous Emmy in mid-2000.

While Shari Lewis was a person of many creative talents—she was an accomplished orchestra conductor and a writer who once coauthored an episode of *Star Trek*—she created a lifelong niche around the same characters that made her famous in the 1950s. But unlike many performers who unsuccessfully keep trying to revive past glories, Lewis didn't have just an act, she had a message. The idea that children were special people who could accomplish anything was her "corporate culture," and this mission was able to sustain the message of a sassy sock puppet for more than three generations.

Whether you are a puppeteer or a global multinational corporation, your best chance of success revolves around keeping true to the core values that first made you successful. This does not mean that inherent natural forces will keep your business out of new markets. Rather, it means that your best prospects for success lie within those markets whose needs match your strengths and values.

Know Who Your Customers Are

Success teaches many lessons. Unfortunately, it can also breed a sense of organizational myopia, where you see things from an internal perspective that may not be shared by the outside world. As a result, it is far too easy for your Midas touch to more closely resemble "The Emperor's New Clothes" when you go to market without the perspective of your customer base—as one baby food manufacturer discovered the hard way.

GERBER GROWN-UP FOOD?

Food manufacturer Gerber has long been the market leader in selling baby food in jars. But one day in the 1970s, it decided to take its concept up-market, and the result was Gerber Singles—dinners for grown-ups in jars. It discovered in short order that buyers didn't want to be publicly branded as single people, and didn't care to dine from packages resembling large containers of Gerber baby food. As author Susan Casey noted in *Business 2.0* magazine, "They might as well have called it I Live Alone and Eat My Meals from a Jar." Undaunted, Gerber pressed on to try marketing its dessert items to teenagers as Gerber Desserts, with the message that "Gerber isn't just for babies anymore." And once again, the market came back and said with unmistakable clarity, "Oh yes, it is."

Product marketing authority Robert McMath often refers to a phenomenon known as "corporate Alzheimer's," where companies repeatedly try new things that have failed in the past by not looking beyond their own internal views of the world. Many organizations succeed by doing something well, and then mistake that success as a universal license to do the same thing in other markets. Conversely, firms who listen to the needs and trends of their customers can tap tremendous synergies as they expand, as FedEx discovered when it added its brand identity to the ground delivery business.

FEDEX TAKES TO THE HIGHWAY

When FedEx acquired the parent firm of trucking giant Roadway Package System in 1998, it marked an important shift in corporate identity, from overnight delivery to a full range of shipping and logistics services. The merger eventually gave Roadway's former operations an instant business identity in the public mind—FedEx Ground—and provided its parent company with a subsidiary that allowed it to move into both business and residential ground package delivery.

This move enabled FedEx to position itself as a legitimate single-source provider of shipping services. The new ground division continues to maintain its own separate operations, under what soon became a corporate philosophy of "operating independently and competing collectively," but has allowed the parent company to provide a seamless range of services under one corporate banner. And today, its investment of more than $2 billion led to double-digit growth rates for its new subsidiary, while boosting the parent company's overall revenues to more than $20 billion per year.

Know Where You Are Going

For many businesses, the riskiest expansion strategy may in fact be the lack of one. Customers and markets rarely stand still, which means that what worked during one snapshot in time may fail in another. Success in the long term requires a constant eye to the future.

The rapid growth of the personal computing era is a perfect example of this need to continually evolve your culture to suit the marketplace. It was a business area that began serving hobbyists and technology professionals, but quickly exploded to become one of the largest business and consumer markets of all time. One aspect of this market, word-processing software, teaches an important lesson in how business culture drove the rise of three major corporations and the subsequent decline of two of them.

THE WORD-PROCESSING WARS

In the early 1980s, the dominant word-processing software was a program known as **Wordstar.** In these fledgling days of personal computing, this program was one of the first "killer apps," unlocking the ability to create documents and publications for a generation of people that was new to using computers. Although it required a cumbersome litany of typed commands to run (at one point spawning a wall poster listing all of them), it quickly became the program of choice for many early PC users.

But soon, Wordstar became a victim of its own success, because of a trend that few people foresaw. Like most software products of its time, Wordstar users needed to contact their dealers for support and assistance. Between the wide network of firms selling this software, and natural incentives to favor sales over service, many users found that their questions were met with shrugged shoulders and a request to read the manual again. As a result, much of its core customer base was composed of the "technologically courageous" who had the wherewithal to figure things out on their own.

Later in the 1980s, a Utah-based company known as **WordPerfect** launched a competitive word-processing product by the same name. It too was a cumbersome, command-based program, but with one crucial difference: it included toll-free support for any licensed user, directly from the company. Suddenly, the market saw a near total shift from technology issues to service ones. Housewives and secretaries were now joining computer hobbyists in doing word processing, a massive consumer industry was born, and WordPerfect's support hotline became so popular that its 5.0 release once caused Utah's single area code to shut down for two full days. In its heyday, WordPerfect even hired live disc jockeys to play music and tell callers how long they could expect to wait on hold for assistance.

A few years later, social and competitive trends turned the market upside down once again, as word processing dropped dramatically in price and could no longer feasibly support unlimited customer assistance. This trend made "ease-of-use" the new buzzword, and this time software giant **Microsoft** was ready with Microsoft Word, a product that dovetailed neatly with its new point-and-click Windows operating system. Today, this product continues to dominate the market for word processing, and helped drive an overall suite of applications software that now represents approximately one-third of Microsoft's annual revenues.

In this case, one company first succeeded with a business culture that served hobbyists and early computer enthusiasts, with an unspoken mantra of "create neat products for people who are smart enough to figure them out." This culture failed to scale upwards to a mass market that needed service as well as lots of cool features. Then, a highly service-oriented culture came to dominate the market, only to fall in turn to another one that valued customer-driven product innovation at a time when the market needed it.

The overarching lesson from each of these areas is that growth into new markets requires a careful assessment of your culture in relationship to this market, and more important, where both you and this market are heading in the future. As you think of expanding the scope of your own organization, think through cultural factors such as:

- How does this new market differ from my own?
- Are we trying to change them?
- Will we have to change to meet their tastes?
- What is the impact of these changes on who we are today?
- Where do we want this new market to lead us?

In a very real sense, growth by market expansion is much like the classic interview question, "What do you plan to be doing in five years?" By thinking through where you want to go in light of your underlying culture, you can choose the kind of growth that lets you be true to who you are, and where you want to be in the future. It would be fair to say that change is the one constant as businesses seek the right ways to grow and expand. But if you remain true to your underlying culture, and listen to your customers in the process, your growth directions can ultimately become another factor that perpetuates the success of that culture.

BUSINESS EXPANSION AND YOUR CULTURE

Expansion can be a risky move for any business. But there are times when not expanding can seem even riskier, particularly when larger players enjoy lower costs and competitive advantages because of economies of scale. At other times expansion represents an opportunity that needs to be seized. And in some cases, you must truly grow or die. The advent of the computer era, for example, vastly changed the fortunes of one typewriter manufacturer, IBM, while it sent others such as Smith-Corona to the corporate graveyard. So the search for new markets and new partners is a never-ending quest for most companies, and particularly so for ones with successful cultures.

At the same time, the stakes can be quite high. Poorly conceived mergers and ill-timed forays into new markets have damaged or even killed many a firm, and those who survive the experience inevitably see their cultures evolve from it—for better or for worse. And even the best of expansion plans involve periods of risk and anxiety, ranging from the effects of a merger on people's jobs to the uneasy anticipation of whether a large investment in a new product or market will pay off. On top of these global issues, expansion represents both an opportunity and a risk for your top performers: even in cultures that are highly tolerant of failure, no one wants the reputation of being behind the next New Coke product or Snapple merger.

It is here, when a culture is most at risk, that its strength is tested the most. Those firms that partner and expand successfully, while remaining true to who they are, often create an infrastructure that, in turn, fuels further growth and success. Others learn from failed expansion schemes, and become more focused on their core markets and values in the future. Either way, the desire to grow beyond the current borders of your business often becomes a defining moment for your culture. Managed well, it often becomes your culture's long-term blueprint for growth and success in the future.

11

Can Corporate Cultures Really Change?

C**an the fundamentals of an** organization ever really change? Perhaps the deeper question is whether people themselves can change. Psychologists feel that human personalities are largely formed by age six and remain remarkably constant throughout our lives. And if we look at specific workplaces, particularly dysfunctional ones, many of them also seem doomed to repeat the same mistakes over and over, as though they, too, were saddled with a lifelong organizational personality. Given the inertia and bureaucracy that can become entrenched in many organizations, can we ever really hope to effect permanent changes in them?

The answer is a definite yes. Just as many people have turned around their personal lives, there is no lack of success stories among businesses that have changed their cultures. Organizational personalities may not be easily changed, and human nature may be stronger than ever, but we all remain capable of both evolutionary and revolutionary change when it is needed. From the largest Fortune 500 boardroom to the smallest workplace, history has proven time and again that business culture can be changed for the better. One very dramatic example of this was the late-1990s turnaround of Continental Airlines, from one of the lowest-ranked major airlines to one of the best in the nation.

A REBIRTH AT CONTINENTAL AIRLINES

One day in 1996, one of the most incredible open letters to customers ever written was published in the in-flight magazine of **Continental Airlines.** Written by CEO Gordon Bethune, it stated plainly in the first paragraph that it had been "a last-place airline." And it bluntly declared that it had long neglected the two things needed for long-term success: having a product it was proud of and people who looked forward to coming to work every day. He then proceeded to detail, in four single-spaced pages of copy, all the things that he and Continental were now doing to change these problems.

The Continental Airlines of the early 1990s was indeed a last-place airline. Its mantra was to do things as cheaply as possible, and it often did rank dead last on industry surveys of on-time arrivals, baggage problems, and customer satisfaction. Financially, it had been through two bankruptcies and five CEOs in the past decade. But when Bethune, a former Navy aircraft mechanic and Boeing manager, took over the helm, things changed radically. New standards were set, new incentives were put in place, a fresh look was taken at routes, services, and market strategy—and even the planes themselves were repainted with a global theme. More important, Bethune openly and constantly communicated a vision of where Continental could lead its market.

These changes were as global as redesigning its operations (to, as Continental president Greg Brenneman put it, "fly to places people wanted to go, and serve food at mealtimes"), and as specific as tripling the frequency of cleaning its aircraft. Painful cuts were made, particularly among the management ranks, but Continental seized this opportunity to bring in fresh leadership at all levels of the company. Its employees were now part of the process. They gained a share of company profits and bonuses for on-time performance, had a live hotline to management for suggestions, and received a weekly voice mail directly from Bethune on the state of the business.

Today, Continental sits at or near the top of its industry rankings, is rated by *Fortune* magazine as one of America's top employers, and has become a preferred carrier for the lucrative business travel market. And its "Go Forward" plan to restructure the carrier as an industry leader is now celebrated as one of the classic business turnaround stories of the past decade.

One of the unique things about Continental's rebirth is that it not only measured success in financial terms, but also by employee metrics such as turnover, sick leave, and accident rates. It knew that it had to come up with an entirely new work environment, which was why creating a culture of trust and respect was one of the four cornerstones of its turnaround plan. And one of the more interesting metrics to emerge from it was that sales of Continental logo merchandise to employees soon increased by a factor of four. (Years earlier, Brenneman, in an incident that he says "still sends chills down my spine," discovered an entire maintenance crew who had ripped the company logo from their uniforms, because they didn't want people outside work to know they were employed by Continental.) Today, Continental receives more than 150,000 employment applications per year, and its annual revenues have grown to nearly $10 billion. Its story serves as a living example that no matter how dysfunctional you once were, a dramatic change in business fortunes can be driven by a change in culture.

THE CATALYSTS OF CULTURE CHANGE

Both human beings and organizations have the capacity to change—and neither process is easy. Business cultures are never static entities but are living processes that learn and change constantly over time. This is why businesses of all sizes grow and evolve into the future, for better and worse, and in both evolutionary and revolutionary ways.

Very often, a culture changes because it has two stark choices—change or die. For example, when Springfield Remanufacturing embarked on its ambitious experiment to open its books to employees and make them part of "the great game" of business success, it wasn't just trying a neat idea that sounded good. It launched a new era of employee ownership to keep its plant from being closed, and employees were just one small financial misstep away from losing all their jobs. While it ultimately became a high-growth firm listed among the 100 Best Companies to Work For, it was raw survival that drove its change from a command-and-control shop floor environment to one of high employee involvement.

Even when the choices are not as stark, many areas of internal pain can drive the change of a culture: productivity, morale, turnover, or quality, to name a few. More important, it takes intelligent leadership to realize when a culture change is the appropriate solution to these problems.

WHEN FRESH THINKING RESCUED THE AMERICAN EXPRESS CARD

When Kenneth Chenault led the consumer card division of **American Express** in the early 1990s, he had inherited an organization whose glory days seemed behind it. Merchants were rebelling against its high fees, competitors such as MasterCard and Visa were taking increasing amounts of market share away from it, and the number of American Express cards in circulation was actually dropping. Chenault's response to this landscape was to take an entrenched bureaucracy and make it start thinking like an innovator. He pushed the division to move away from its niche market of high-end cardholders and into aggressive moves such as frequent-flier programs, co-branded cards with stores and airlines, and acceptance by a much broader mass market of retailers. By the end of the decade, card revenues had tripled, and Chenault was eventually named the company's new CEO in early 2001.

Here once again, the fundamental conflict between human nature and organizational values drives how people respond to these points of pain. One organization might attack productivity problems by creating more rules and pressuring people to work harder, while another might create an environment that focuses on innovation and results. In the first case, the side effects on employee morale and commitment may never even factor into the equation, causing a death spiral that exacerbates the problems it was trying to solve in the first place. This is why people who think through their cultural values, and their long-term implications, are often at such a strong competitive advantage over the vast majority who simply do what seems obvious when problems arise.

In the case of American Express, there are still myriad new challenges on the horizon: a slowing economy and a severely depressed travel sector as of this writing have hit hard at its core business areas. But Chenault still publicly casts these problems as opportunities to build a stronger and more diversified company for the long term, as it pursues growth areas in global financial and payment services. Above all, compared with the American Express of a decade ago, its stuffy past is gone for good—and as Chenault recently told his employees, "I represent the best company and the best people in the world."

Perhaps the other good reason for culture change is new leadership or partnership. Every change of leadership represents a culture change, for better or for worse. Whether it is caused by succession, turnover, or takeover, new management brings with it a new set of values.

Ironically, leaders alone cannot change a culture—that is ultimately in the hands of every person in an organization. This is why some leaders often exhort their employees to change, and don't get results. What is really true, however, is that leaders often determine what kinds of people an organization hires and the day-to-day policies that drive its operations. These people and these policies, in turn, ultimately determine the corporate culture. When the right kind of leader is able to come in and implement these changes, within an organization that is ready to change, the results can be dramatic, as the growth of longtime clothing retailer Christopher & Banks recently demonstrated.

CHRISTOPHER & BANKS—SUCCEEDING BY KEEPING "MARY" HAPPY

One of the hottest stocks of the year 2000 was not a high-flying dot-com company or a merger of corporate titans. It was an old-line retail chain of women's clothing stores that has been around since 1956. **Christopher & Banks,** whose fashions are aimed at the baby-boom generation, has seen its stock increase more than 8,800 percent in the five years from 1995–2000, making it the most successful growth stock during that period.

The chain's future was once far from rosy. By its 40th anniversary in 1996, when it was known as Braun's Fashions, it was mired in bankruptcy court after years of selling drab, low-priced women's clothing in an increasingly crowded marketplace. But two years later, by the time general merchandising manager William Prange took over as CEO, a culture change was underfoot. The chain remodeled its stores, changed its name to match one of its clothing labels, improved service quality, and focused on the largely underserved market segment of 35- to 55-year-old women. It even invented a fictitious model customer named "Mary," a 45-year-old soccer mom living with two children in suburbia, and used her tastes and habits to guide its business model. Christopher & Banks executives even go so far as to shop and vacation in places that Mary would frequent.

Today, Christopher & Banks is growing strongly from its roots in the Midwest, and more recently it added a new line of stores aimed at the plus-size market. Financially, it remains a popular stock with a market capitalization of more than half a billion dollars. More important, it proved that even a tired old retail clothing chain could succeed in a big way by changing its focus.

Workplaces of any size are transformed every day by changes in culture, leadership, or other factors. I was once involved in managing a customer-support center that changed within a year from 20 percent turnover and fair-to-middling customer satisfaction to near zero turnover and near perfect customer ratings, with largely the same team of people. To be sure, many factors were at work behind this, including better equipment, more automation, and improved operating procedures. But perhaps the most important change had nothing to do with any of these things. We fostered a new set of values that customer support was an important profession and backed it up with expanded training, professional activities, and an outreach role to the rest of the organization.

All organizations face problems and upheavals in their existence, just like people do. So what is the difference between those organizations who leverage them as a catalyst to change their culture and those who do not? Sometimes, it is simply a matter of the right people being in the right place at the right time—Continental Airlines, for example, did not fundamentally address many of its problems until the latest in a long line of CEOs decided that a culture change was key to resolving them. Until this person came along, neither bankruptcies nor changes in leadership motivated the need to make the same kinds of changes. And some organizations remain blind to the fact that a culture change is required at all, and they ride their dysfunctional cultures straight out of existence. Either way, the desire to change is never just driven by external events, it starts on the inside, with who you are. And ultimately, the ability to change when needed is perhaps the most important cultural trait of all.

YOU HAVE THE POWER

While *corporate culture* has become a fashionable term to describe the core values that drive an organization, it is also very misleading, because *corporate* implies that business culture is purely the domain of large corporations and high-flying CEOs. It also implies a certain powerlessness on the part of the individual. In reality, neither could be further from the truth.

Every organization, of any size, has its own culture, and its leaders exert tremendous influence over the values that drive that culture. This is equally true if you are a global multinational corporation, a small department of a larger company, or a family business. You personally have the power to define the values behind your own working environment. You also have the power to change the values your workplace currently follows. And the ripple effect of defining and improving these values can move mountains, in your work and in your life.

ONE PERSON CAN MAKE
A BILLION-DOLLAR DIFFERENCE

In the early 1980s, a young computer programmer in a sleepy California engineering consulting firm convinced his bosses to let him try to turn their own crude programs into a commercially viable software package for designing products. He hired a small number of people, including me, convinced a computer manufacturer to loan him an expensive minicomputer in exchange for a revenue stake, and proceeded to launch a product that soon helped define the red-hot global market for computer-aided design (CAD) software. Despite competition that included major aerospace and computing firms, his company outmaneuvered them by focusing on values that others did not: high commitment, consistently excellent service, and continuous technical growth. Today, more than 20 years later, this product has generated nearly a billion dollars in lifetime revenues.

The important point of this story is that many companies eventually set out on the same path as this one, but the unspoken values behind this one created something that was almost magical. There was a clear difference between this firm and its competitors that would never show up on paper, but emerged with unmistakable clarity on its balance sheet. In a very real sense, this book has been written to bottle up the magic behind values like these, and to hand it to you in a game plan that can be put to work today in your own organization.

By understanding that your culture drives your success, you have joined a very exclusive fraternity—those who realize that you can create unthinkable levels of success, and touch people's lives, on the wings of something that most people never even discuss. Building a successful corporate culture goes beyond business processes and into being a way of life. It gives meaning and purpose to the place where most of us spend over half of our waking lives. More important, it reduces the vast complexities of the business world into a clear sense of who you are and where you are headed. It is truly the soul of your organization.

References

CHAPTER 1: Understanding Your Business Culture

Covey, Stephen. *Seven Habits of Highly Effective People.* Fireside Press, 1990.

Katzenbach, Jon R., and Jason A. Santamaria. "Firing Up the Front Line." *Harvard Business Review,* 1 May 1999, 107.

Peters, Thomas, and Robert H. Waterman. *In Search of Excellence.* Warner Books, 1982.

CHAPTER 2: The Strategists: Driving Operational Excellence

"About Vanguard: Unmatchable Excellence." The Vanguard Group, <www.vanguard .com>, 2000.

Barrett, Amy, and Jeffrey M. Laderman. "That's Why They Call It Vanguard: It Pioneered Index Funds—and Now It's Outpacing Its Rivals." *Business Week,* 18 January 1999.

"Best Buy Co., Inc., Hires New Vice President; New VP of Enterprise CRM Named." *Business Wire,* 10 December 2001.

"Best Buy Creates Alliance with Partsearch Technologies to Develop Master Parts Catalog for Industry." *Business Wire,* 27 November 2001.

Brooker, Katrina. "I Built This Company, I Can Save It." *Business 2.0,* April 2001.

Carlsen, Clifford. "Krispy Kreme to Make Dough in Bay Area." *San Francisco Business Times,* 19 June 1998.

"Company Profiles: Vanguard Group." <www.vault.com>, 2000.

Creswell, Julie. "Remedies for an Economic Hangover." *Fortune,* 25 June 2001.

Davis, Nick, Carlotta Grandstaff, and Ken Picard. "Toss Here Missoula." *Missoula Independent,* 6 December 2001.

Kohn, Alfie. "For Best Results, Forget the Bonus." *New York Times,* 17 October 1993.

LaBounty, Char. "Beware what you measure!" *Service News,* November 1996.

"LensCrafters Moves to Top 50 on Fortune Magazine's List of 100 Best Companies to Work For in America," LensCrafters, Inc., press release, 18 December 2000.

Nelson, Bob. "Energizing Teams of Hourly Workers." *Bob Nelson's Rewarding Employees* newsletter, 1 May 1999, <www.nelson-motivation.com>.

"Our Background," LensCrafters, Inc., <www.lenscrafters.com>.

Sittenfeld, Curtis. "Job Titles of the Future: Minister of Culture." *Fast Company,* 17 (September 1998): 64.

Walton, Mary. *The Deming Management Method.* New York: Putnam Publishing Group, 1986, 6.

Zall, Milton. "Pluses and Minuses of Variable Pay." American Chemical Society, *Today's Chemist at Work,* 10: 8 (September 2001).

CHAPTER 3: The Motivators: Creating a Positive Working Environment

Coghlan, Jeff. Wendcentral (Wendy's franchisee), personal interview, used with permission, March 2002.

"Corporate Fact Sheet." Wendy's International, Inc.—Investor Relations, <www.wendysinvest.com>.

Greenwald, Gerald, and Charles Madigan. *Lessons from the Heart of American Business: A Roadmap for Managers in the 21st Century.* Warner Books, February 2001.

Hildebrand, Carol. "Satisfaction Guaranteed: Insurer USAA understands that serving customers well doesn't mean that things will never go wrong but being willing and able to respond when they do." *CIO,* August 1995.

Kroeker, Wally. "The High Cost of Dissent." Mennonite Economic Development Associates, *MEDA News,* Spring 1999, <www.meda.org>.

Levering, Robert, and Milton Moskowitz. *The 100 Best Companies to Work For in America.* Plume, 1994, 456–461 (USAA).

MacKenzie, Gordon. *Orbiting the Giant Hairball: A Corporate Fool's Guide to Surviving with Grace.* Viking, April 1998.

Masie, Ellliott. "Where Is Learning on the Radar Screen Today?" <www.masie.com>, 14 December 2001.

Shah, Jennifer Baljko. "FedEx's hub of supply chain activity." CMP Media, Inc., *EBN,* 10 May 2001.

Thomas, R.D. *Dave's Way,* Berkley Publishing, 1992.

Toy Story (movie), John Lasseter, director. Buena Vista/Pixar, 1995.

Uttal, Bro, with Edward C. Baig and Cynthia Hutton. "Managing Companies That Serve You Best: Customer Coddling Is the Hot New Competitive Weapon." *Fortune,* 7 December 1987, 98.

Welles, Edward O. "The People Business." *Inc,* 15 October 1999.

"Wendy's Story." Wendy's International, Inc., <www.wendys.com>.

CHAPTER 4: The Team Builders: Getting the Best from Your Human Capital

Charney, Reginald B. "High-Tech Hiring Practices: A View from the Trenches." *Dr. Dobb's Journal,* Spring 1999.

Colvin, Geoffrey. "Smile! It's Recession Time! No one likes a bad economy, but it must be hard for these four fortunate guys not to gloat." *Fortune,* 29 October 2001, 48.

"Fact Sheet: Source2Hire," Development Dimensions International, Inc., <www .ddiworld.com>.

Freiberg, Kevin, and Jackie Freiberg. *Nuts! Southwest Airlines' Crazy Recipe for Business and Personal Success.* Bard Press, 1996.

Johnson, Cathy. "Grass Roots Leadership for the New World of Business." <www .loma.org>, December 2000.

Kane, Kate. "The Riddle of Job Interviews." *Fast Company,* November 1995.

Leibs, Scott. "Help Wanted (And How)—Information Technology Staff Shortages." *CFO,* November 2000.

Levering, Robert, and Milton Moskowitz. *The 100 Best Companies to Work For in America.* Plume, 1994, 480–483 (Wegmans).

McCann, Hugh. "Straight Talk in Teamland. (Team Development in Auto Industry.)" *Ward's Auto World,* 32 (1 February 1996): 27.

Melymuka, Kathleen. "Sky King." *Computerworld,* 28 September 1998.

Puffer, Sheila M. "Continental Airlines' CEO Gordon Bethune on Teams and New Product Development." *The Academy of Management Executive,* 13 (1 August 1999): 28–35.

"Recruiting Q&A: Intrawest's Chris Wrazej." *BusinessWeek Online,* 5 December 2000.

"Retaining Experienced CSRs at Time-Warner Memphis," case study. State Technical Institute at Memphis, TEFATE team, June 1999.

"Southwest Airlines—Fact Sheet." Southwest Airlines, Inc., <www.southwest .com>, 4 March 2002.

Tracy, Diane, and William J. Morin. *Truth, Trust and the Bottom Line: 7 Steps to Trust-Based Management.* Dearborn Trade Publishing, 2001.

World-Class Courtesy: A Best Practices Report. National Performance Review, 1997.

CHAPTER 5: The Nimble: Building an Infrastructure for Change

"AutoNation Profit Rises on Sales Strength." *Reuters Business Report,* 7 February 2002.

Bananas (movie). Woody Allen, director. United Artists, 1971.

Brenneman, Greg. "Right Away and All at Once: How We Saved Continental." *Harvard Business Review,* 1 September 1998, 162.

Dicksteen, Lisa Napell. "Almost Human." *Customer Support Management,* 1 November 2001.

Harding, Elizabeth U. "No Scheduling Blues for JetBlue Home-based Agents." <www.zdnet.com>, 1 June 2001.

Jones, Del, and Barbara Hansen. "Special Report: A Who's Who of Productivity." *USA Today,* 30 August 2001, 1B.

Kim, W. Chan, and Renée Mauborgne. "When 'Competitive Advantage' Is Neither." *The Wall Street Journal* (Europe), 21 April 1997.

McGraw, Dan. "Will He Own the Road?" *U.S. News & World Report,* 123 (20 October 1997): 44.

MacKenzie, Gordon. *Orbiting the Giant Hairball: A Corporate Fool's Guide to Surviving with Grace.* Viking, April 1998.

O'Herron, Jennifer. "Paving the Road for Travelers." *Call Center,* 14 July 2000.

O'Reilly, Brian. "They've Got Mail!" *Fortune,* 7 February 2000.

Orwell, George. *Animal Farm: A Fairy Story.* Alfred Knopf, 1946.

Powell, Barbara. "AutoNation Strives for a Second Chance." *South Florida Sun-Sentinel,* 13 June 2001.

Walters, Dottie, and Lilly Walters. *Speak and Grow Rich.* Prentice-Hall, 1989, 26–27.

Walker, John, Editor. "The Autodesk File: Bits of History, Words of Experience," Fourth Edition. <www.fourmilab.ch/autofile>, 1994.

Witsil, Frank. "Ft. Lauderdale, Fla.–Based AutoNation Undergoes Overhaul to Drive Sales. *Tampa Tribune,* 15 January 2002.

CHAPTER 6: The Customer Champions: Building a Service Culture

Bowen, David E., and Edward E. Lawler, III. "Empowering service employees." *Sloan Management Review* 36 (22 June 1995): 73(12).

Chenault, Kenneth I. Lewis H. Durland Memorial Lecture. Cornell University, Ithaca, NY, 17 October 2001.

Dell, Michael, with Catherine Fredman. *Direct from Dell: Strategies That Revolutionized an Industry.* HarperBusiness, 1999.

Fierman, Jaclyn. "Americans Can't Get No Satisfaction." *Fortune,* 11 December 1995.

Fishman, Charles. "Face Time with Michael Dell." *Fast Company,* 1 March 2001, 82.

"Gore Touts Customer Service Commitments of 10 Agencies; Launches 'Conversations with America' to Hear from Americans," Office of the Vice President, The White House, 2 March 1998.

"Modernising Public Services Group Standards of Service." <www.cabinet-office .gov.uk>, March 2000.

"Nordstrom Takes the Hassle Out of Returns." ZDNet E-Commerce Best Practices Evaluation, 7 December 1999, <www.zdnet.com>.

Pine, B. Joseph II, Don Peppers, and Martha Rogers. "Do You Want to Keep Customers Forever?" *Harvard Business Review,* 1 March 1995, 103.

Stewart, Thomas A. "A Satisfied Customer Isn't Enough." *Fortune,* 21 July 1997.

Sussman, Diane. "Hospital Food Is Improving. Really." *Nurseweek,* 15 May 2000.

Vernon, Lillian. "Make Someone Happy—Your Customer." EntreWorld.org, 1 July 1998.

CHAPTER 7: The Passionate: Business as a Way of Life

Bigbee, Ivy. "The New Greatest Show on Earth: Cirque du Soleil 'La Nouba' Is Stellar Attraction at Disney." <www.ivybigbee.com>.

Brooker, Katrina. "The Best Little Oil House in Texas." *Fortune,* 3 September 2001.

"Cirque du Monde," brochure. Cirque du Soleil, July 2000.

Collins, James C. "Turning Goals into Results: The Power of Catalytic Mechanisms." *Harvard Business Review,* 1 July 1999, 70.

"4th Annual Great Paper Airplane Contest." Telemetry, AIAA Alabama-Mississippi section, <www.msfc.nasa.gov/AIAA>, January 1998.

Frank, B.J. "Born into the Business: Work ethic, dedication, and persistence pass from generation to generation (Shop profile: Opeka Auto Repair)," *AutoInc.* XLV: 9 (September 1997).

"Great Job/Video-Game Expert: Meet a Real Game Boy—He Helps Nintendo Players Get Out of Jams." *Time for Kids,* 18 September 1998, 7.

Hall, Cheryl. "Magical Mystery Tour: Ringmasters Turn a Circus into an Empire." *The Dallas Morning News,* 8 February 1998, 1H.

Hamm, Steve. "Online Original: Capellas: From Gridiron to Podium to Home." *Business Week Online,* 4 September 2000.

Holloway, Nigel. "Profiles: Agora." Forbes Global, Forbes.com, 30 October 2000, <www.forbes.com/global/2000/1030/0322086a.html>.

Jameson, J. "Cirque Du Sensational." *The Courier-Mail* (Brisbane, Australia), 23 January 1999, 1.

Johnson, Brian D. "Cirque Du Success: The Montreal circus has reached the top with a mix of ethereal athletics and business savvy." *Maclean's,* 27 July 1998, 36.

Lambert, Catherine. "Language of Diversity." *Sunday Herald Sun* (Melbourne, Australia), 21 February 1999, 67.

Loewe, Marianne (Concern America). Personal interview, used with permission, May 2000.

Munk, Nina. "A High-Wire Act." *Forbes,* 22 September 1997, 192.

Paine, Lynn Sharp. "Managing for Organizational Integrity." *Harvard Business Review,* 1 March 1994, 106.

Pospisil, Vivian. *Broken Promises: An Unconventional View of What Went Wrong at IBM.* (Book review.) *Industry Week* 245 (19 August 1996): 106(1).

Spener, David. "The Freirean Approach to Adult Literacy Education." National Clearinghouse for ESL Literacy Education (NCLE), April 1990.

"A Word from Our Founding President," Guy Laliberté. <www.cirquedusoleil.com>.

CHAPTER 8: The Visionaries: Leadership That Seeks a Higher Purpose

Arpi, Rich, and Joe Block. "Baseball, Minnesota: The Northern League." <www.spsaints.com>, 2001.

Berry, Leonard. *Discovering the Soul of Service: The Nine Drivers of Sustainable Business Success.* Free Press, 1999, 27–33, 52–54.

Charan, Ram, and Geoffrey Colvin. "Why CEOs Fail: It's rarely for lack of smarts or vision. Most unsuccessful CEOs stumble because of one simple, fatal short-coming." *Fortune,* 21 June 1999, 68.

Chenault, Kenneth I. Lewis H. Durland Memorial Lecture. Cornell University, Ithaca, NY, 17 October 2001.

Greco, Susan. "Saints Alive!" *Inc,* 1 August 2001.

Mills, Richard. Speech at New York State Department of Education Leadership Conference, SUNY-Oswego, May 2001.

Moody, John. Fox News Channel, personal interview, used with permission, January 2002.

"Our Credo," Johnson and Johnson. <www.jnj.com>, used by permission.

Roberts, Kate. "Wendy's Founder Dave Thomas Dies." Associated Press, 8 January 2002.

"Saint for a Summer Archives." <www.spsaints.com>, 2001.

Stack, Jack, and Bo Burlingham. *The Great Game of Business.* Currency/Double-day, October 1994.

CHAPTER 9: Why Do Corporate Cultures Fail?

"Company History." The Great Atlantic and Pacific Tea Company, <www.aptea .com>.

"European Airlines in Crisis." CNN.com, 3 October 2001

Greenwald, John. "Peterman Reboots: The quirky catalog owner lost everything, including his name, by overexpanding. Now he's back and plans to get big slowly." *Time,* 20 August 2001.

Kotter, John, and James Hesket. *Corporate Culture and Performance.* Free Press, 1992.

Patton, Susannah. "Can IT Save A&P, the Granddaddy of Grocery Chains?" *CIO,* 15 February 2001.

Vlasic, Bill, and David Phillips. "GM pours $1.5 billion into Saturn." *The Detroit News,* 26 April 2000.

CHAPTER 10: Cultural Due Diligence: Mergers, Acquisitions, and Other Growth Strategies

"Bear Stearns Settles Suit on Bad Merger Advice." Reuters Business Report, 8 August 2000.

Casey, Susan."Object Oriented: Everything I Ever Needed to Know about Business I Learned in the Frozen-Food Aisle." *Business 2.0,* October 2000.

Castaneda, Laura."Southwest Purchases Morris—$134 Mllion Stock Swap Finalizes Deal." *Dallas Morning News,* 1 January 1994.

"Chase-Pitkin History," *Chase-Pitkin Home and Garden,* <www.chase-pitkin.com>.

Creswell, Julie. "First: Killer Deals: When Bad Mergers Happen to Good Firms." *Fortune,* 1 May 2000, 46.

Fonti, Nancy. "Heated Pilot Talks a 'Sea Change' for Delta." *The Atlanta Journal-Constitution,* 25 February 2001.

Gardner, Jim. "Editor's Notebook: Sobering Report on Mergers & Accusations." *San Francisco Business Times,* 17 January 1997.

Grant, Linda. "Why FedEx Is Flying High." *Business 2.0,* November 1997.

Halbrooks, John R. "Of Machines and Mergers." 1999 Fitness Industry Technology, IHRSA, 1999.

Higgins, Amy. "Delta Family Has Grown Dysfunctional." *The Cincinnati Enquirer,* 15 April 2001.

Jindel, Satish. "Putting Service Before Savings." *Traffic World,* 15 October 2001.

Kass, Rochelle. "Michael Weinstein: Westchester Business Leader of the Year." *The Journal News* (White Plains, NY), 25 March 2001.

Keel, Frank J. "Stern Warning: Holding Your Brands Hostage." *Philadelphia Business Journal,* 10 October 1997.

Labich, Kenneth, and Ani Hadjian. "Is Herb Kelleher America's Best CEO? Behind his clowning is a people-wise manager who wins where others can't." *Fortune,* 2 May 1994, 44.

"Legendary Children's Entertainer Shari Lewis Dies of Cancer." PBS news release, <www.pbs.org>, 3 August 1998.

Levering, Robert, and Milton Moskowitz. *The 100 Best Companies to Work For in America.* Plume, 1994, 151–156 (W.L. Gore), 187–91 (Honda).

"Liquid Asset Rehired: Snapple Queen Wendy Kaufman Savors the Taste of Revenge." *People,* 30 June 1997, 92.

McMath, Robert M., and Thom Forbes. *What Were They Thinking?* Times Books, January 1998.

Menzies, David. "Fabulous Food Flops." *Food in Canada* 58 (1 May 1998): 36(3).

Reck, Virginia P. "Organizational Due Diligence: The Key to Profitable Mergers and Acquisitions." *InTouch On-line Journal,* <intouch.3com.com>, November 1999.

Thornton, Emily, Kathleen Kerwin, et al. "International Business: Japan: Can Honda Go It Alone?" *Business Week* 3636 (5 July 1999) 42.

Tomlinson, Heather. "The Lowdown: Stop Me and Buy a Ben & Jerry's." *Independent on Sunday,* 9 December 2001, 7.

"Why too many mergers miss the mark." *The Economist,* 4 January 1997.

CHAPTER 11: Can Corporate Cultures Really Change?

Bethune, Gordon, and Greg Brenneman. "Special Report: To Our Co-workers, Customers, and Shareholders." *Profiles* (Continental Airlines magazine), Cadmus Custom Publishing, June 1996.

Birger, Jon. "The Best Stock You've Never Heard Of: It's Up 8,800% in Five Years. No, It's not a Tech Stock." *Money,* 1 June 2001.

Brenneman, Greg. "Right Away and All at Once: How We Saved Continental." *Harvard Business Review,* 1 September 1998, 162.

Byrne, John A., and Heather Timmons. "Tough Times for a New CEO." *Business Week,* 29 October 2001, 64.

Chenault, Kenneth I. Lewis H. Durland Memorial Lecture. Cornell University, Ithaca, NY, 17 October 2001.

Price, Dave. "Christopher & Banks Stays on a Roll." *Finance & Commerce,* Dolan Media, 14 December 2000.

Schwartz, Nelson D. "American Express: What's in the Card for Amex?" *Fortune,* 22 January 2001.

Stack, Jack, and Bo Burlingham. *The Great Game of Business.* Currency/Doubleday, October 1994.

Index

ABOUT THE AUTHOR

Rich Gallagher is a leading authority on customer service and support operations. His four previous books include *Smile Training Isn't Enough,* an alternate selection of the Executive Program Book Club, and *Delivering Legendary Customer Service: Seven Steps to Success.* He publishes frequently within the business trade press, and his lengthy management career includes helping to lead a West Coast software start-up to become a major Nasdaq firm as its director of customer services. Visit Rich online at <www.rsgallagher.com>, and for more information on values and corporate culture, visit this book's Web site at <www.SoulOfAnOrganization.com>.

For information on corporate training programs and materials based on *The Soul of an Organization,* contact:

Skills Development International
P.O. Box 4023
Ithaca, NY 14852-4023
E-mail: info@sditrain.com

**Feed Soul Food to
Your Entire Organization!**

For special discounts on
10 or more copies of
The Soul of an Organization,
call Dearborn Trade Special Sales
at 800-621-9621, ext. 4410,
or e-mail rowland@dearborn.com.
You'll receive great service and
top discounts.

For added visibility,
consider private labeling
of books with your
organization name and logo.
We will also help you
identify speakers to make
your next event a
huge success.